THINKING  HISTORY

JON NICHOL

MEDIEVAL REALMS

Contents

2- 3	Thinking Medieval History	
4- 5	The Medieval World	

THE NORMAN CONQUEST AND SETTLEMENT

6- 7	England - 1066
8- 9	Who were the Normans?
10-11	Harold, William or Hardrada?
12-13	The Norman Invasion
14-15	The Battle of Hastings
16-17	William and England, 1066-86
18-19	Castles and Knights
20-21	Domesday Book

RULERS AND PEOPLE - THE MEDIEVAL MONARCHY

22-23	The Feudal System
24-25	Death in the Cathedral
26-27	Henry II, 1154-89
28-29	Crusader!
30-31	King John, 1199-1216
32-33	Magna Carta
34-35	Parliament
36-37	The Peasants' Revolt
38-39	Joan of Arc
40-41	The Wars of the Roses
42-43	Murder!
44-45	The Battle of Bosworth

WALES AND SCOTLAND

46-48	Edward I and Wales
49-50	Concentric Castle
51	Owain Glyndwr
52-53	Edward I and Scotland
54-55	Bannockburn

THE MEDIEVAL VILLAGE

56-57	The Medieval Village
58-59	The Villagers
60-61	The Village Economy
62-63	The Farming Year
64-65	Rainald, Lord of the Manor
66-67	The Lady of the Manor

TOWNS AND TRADE

68-69	The Medieval Town
70-71	The Town Charter
72-73	Market Day
74-75	Jobs - the Town Guilds
76-77	Medieval Trade

THE MEDIEVAL CHURCH

78-80	The Norman Church
81	The Friar
82-83	The Priest
84-85	Monks and Nuns
86-88	Monastery!
89	The Monastic School

SOCIETY

90-91	The Medieval Doctor
92-93	The Black Death 1348
94-95	Crime and Punishment
96	Norman French and English
97	Medieval Timelines - History Quiz
Back cover	Timechart

Thinking Medieval History

Look at picture **A**. I chose it because it is perhaps the most famous picture in British History. What do you know about it? The picture is a great place to start learning about what went on in the past. Can any of you tell the story shown in the picture? Are we sure we know what went on?

Scene **A** tells us about the death of King Harold of England. King Harold died at the Battle of Hastings in 1066. Harold was fighting Duke William of Normandy who had just invaded England from Normandy, part of modern France. Look at the Activity, *King Harold's Death*, and think about what it asks you to do before you go on reading.

a The words on the picture are in Latin, the language of the Romans. The Normans still used Latin to write things down. Below the picture are the words in English. Try and work out what the Latin means.

b Do you think King Harold is the man below the word HAROLD? Or is he the man falling to the ground below INTERFECTUS EST?

c Harold was the last Anglo-Saxon king. The Anglo-Saxon army fought in a long line of footsoldiers. They carried shields, spears, swords and axes, **B**. Now look back at **A**. Are the three men on the left and the four on the right in **A** part of that battle line? The Normans fought on horseback.

d The pictures are from the Bayeux Tapestry. A Norman lord, Odo of Bayeux, had the tapestry made about 20 years after the battle. Historians think it may have been made in Kent, where Odo lived at the time.

The pictures **A** and **B** are the first sources I ask you to think about. I picked the sources in this book because I felt they were the best

EST = IS   HIC = HERE   INTERFECTUS = KILLED   REX = KING

clues for you to use to find out about the past. This book is very much my own view of the past. I hope that you will use it, with the help of your teacher, to make up your own mind about what went on by THINKING your own History. THINKING HISTORY should be fun. It will ask you to think hard while you look, read, talk, write and work on a range of activities.

Why bother to learn about the Middle Ages, a period that lasted about 500 years, from AD 1000-1500? The Middle Ages began at a time when Saxons and Vikings ruled Britain. Then, in 1066, Britain was invaded and conquered for the last time. The invaders were the Normans, led by William the Conqueror. The Middle Ages ended in 1485, when a new ruling family called the Tudors took over the English throne. The Tudors were able to take over because they won at the end of 50 years of Civil War, called the Wars of the Roses.

My reason for studying these 500 years is the impact it still has on all our lives. For example, I can think of many pieces of evidence which still show the impact of the Normans. There are things like personal names. How many Williams, Emmas, Richards or Eleanors do you know? The words we use are a mixture of Norman French and Anglo-Saxon; for instance knife, or servant. The streets of many of our old towns are laid out as they were in the Middle Ages, even if most of the buildings are new. Parliament, which rules our lives, and the English law courts started in the Middle Ages. In THINKING HISTORY you can go back in time, and work out what happened and why. We will look first at what medieval people thought about their world, and then study the Norman Conquest.

King Harold's Death

a Looking at the picture (AT3). Take a small part of the picture, A. Write down three things you can see in it. As a class discuss what you spotted - you will be amazed at how many things you find.
b What the source means (AT3). Read the words below the picture. Now answer the question - how do you think King Harold died? You can discuss this in pairs or as a class.
c King Harold's death (AT1). Write down your thoughts, using the heading 'King Harold's Death'. Or draw your own cartoon of the scene, based on what you know.

ACTIVITY

The Medieval World

Is the world flat or a sphere? What are its continents called and how many are there? What kinds of people and animals live in it? What is its most important city? If you had visited an English king's court between 1000 and 1500 AD, what answers might you have been given to these questions?

To find out I would like us to look at a medieval map of the world, the famous Mappa Mundi, which now hangs in Hereford Cathedral. A medieval priest, Richard de Bello (c1230-1310) made the map. Richard was English, and a Christian. He drew his map to show the world to other Christians. Do you think the map would have looked the same if it had been drawn by a Muslim, or by a Hindu? **A** is the Mappa Mundi's outline. **B** shows some pictures from it, while the Activity, *Medieval Map Maker*, asks you to draw your own Medieval World based on ideas from it. If you turn the Mappa Mundi outline on its side you can work out more easily where the places are.

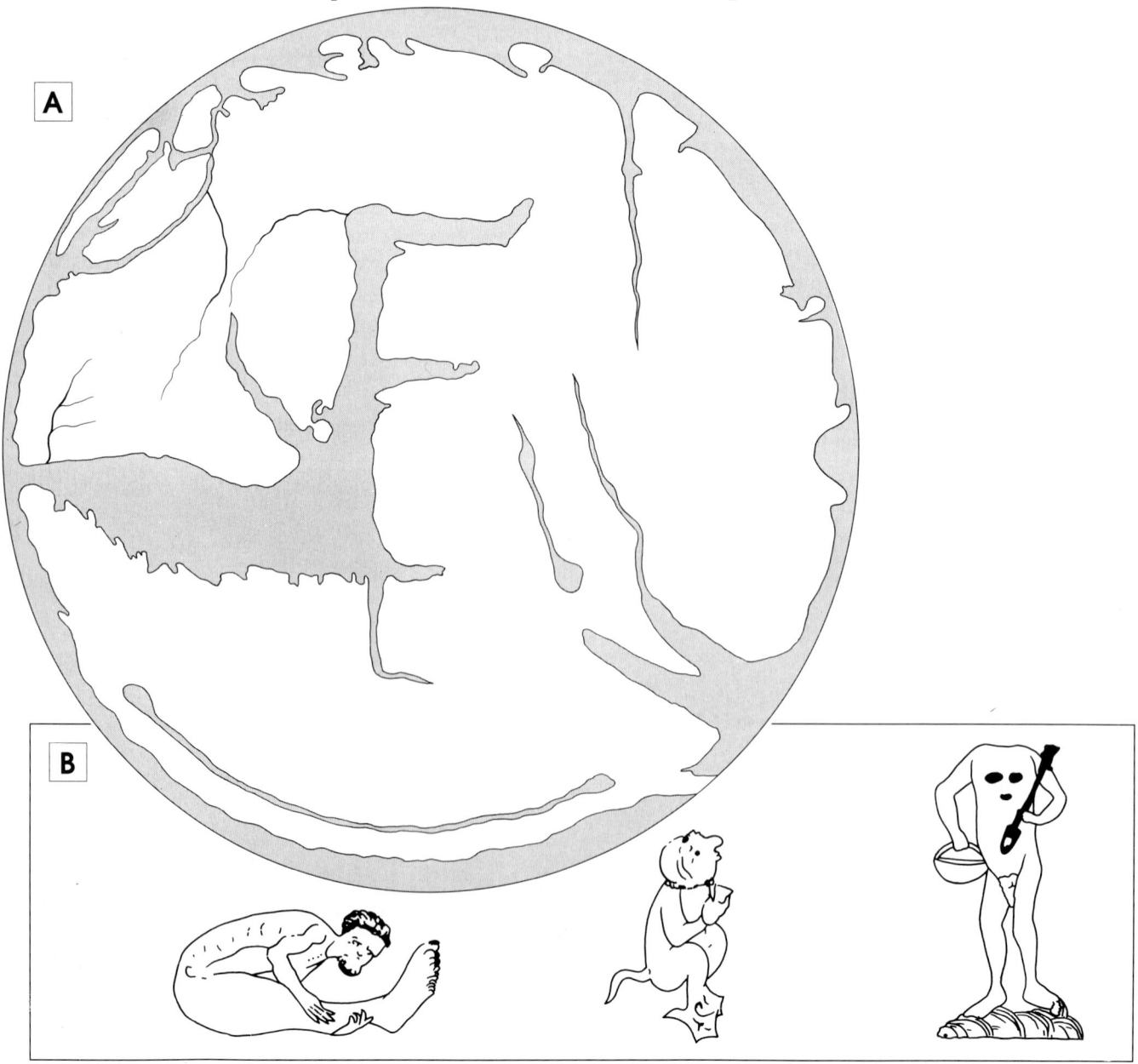

Medieval Map Maker

You can create your own map of the Medieval World. Work by yourself, in pairs or small groups. As a pair or group, split the tasks up between you, drawing different features and sticking them on your master map. You can use a modern atlas to help you. Do rough work in pencil.

1 Drawing the Map (AT2, AT3).
a The World circle. First of all draw a large circle. Put Jerusalem at the centre, and draw the sea all around the edge, see **A**. Why do you think Richard put Jerusalem in the centre?
b The points of the compass. Split the world up into four quarters with East at the top, South on the right, West at the bottom and North on the left.
c Judgment Day. Above the world circle put a picture of Judgment Day, when the world ends and Jesus Christ decides whether you will go to Heaven or Hell. Jesus, the judge, sits on his throne, with Hell to his left and Heaven on his right. Would you have drawn this if you were Muslim?
d The World. Look at **A**. The Mediterranean sea is the roughly T-shaped sea below the centre. The T splits the world up into three parts, Asia at the top, Europe on the bottom left and Africa on the bottom right. Draw the Mediterranean and mark the three continents. The British Isles are on the bottom left hand edge. The Holy Land, which we now call the Middle East, is particularly big on the Mappa Mundi. Why do you think this is?
Did Richard miss anything out? If so why?
e Countries and Scenes. Mark the following:
ASIA
At the top of your map draw a picture of the Garden of Eden, with Adam and Eve. This represents the start of human life.
Palestine, the area around Jerusalem, a picture of Christ being crucified.
Asia Minor (now called Turkey) to the left of Palestine. Draw Noah's Ark high and dry on Mount Ararat.
Babylon, above Palestine, with a picture of the tower of Babel.
Egypt, to the right of Palestine, with a drawing of the pyramids and the Sphinx. Mark the Nile and the Nile's delta.
India, top of Asia, below the Garden of Eden.
China, to the left of India on the other side of a mountain range.
Arabia, to the right of India. Put in the Persian Gulf and the Tigris and Euphrates rivers.

AFRICA
Inland desert, mountains and wild people. Why did Richard think Africa was full of wild people? Also mark the Nile which runs the length of Africa into a lake. From there it goes underground, and pops up again in Asia Minor from where it flows to Egypt.

EUROPE (the shapes are squeezed in, unlike the modern outline)
Try to mark where the modern countries Spain, Italy, Greece, France and Germany are. Off the coast, mark England, Scotland, Wales and Ireland. Scandinavia is above the British Isles.
Russia is above Scandinavia, marked by a bear. The rivers are the main feature - the Danube, Rhine and Rhone, rising in the Alps. Why do you think the rivers were so important to the medieval map maker?
f Animals and People. Your map should have on it many amazing animals and people. Make a choice from the list, or make up your own!

SPECIES	PLACE	FEATURES
Amazons	Asia	Deadly women warriors
Ants	Africa	Giant gold digging ants
Basilisk	Africa	Head of a cockerel, body of a serpent. Breathes a deadly fire
Batmen	Asia	Men with giant ears they wrap around their bodies
Creepermen	Asia	Men with crawling legs, which they creep along on
Dogmen	Norway	Men with dog's heads
Dragons	India	
Griffin	Asia	Head of an eagle, body of a lion
Mermaid	Mediterranean	
Sciapod	India	Men with one huge foot, which they use as a sunshade
Unicorn	Egypt	Body of a deer, single long horn from its head

2 Displaying and judging the maps (AT2). Hold an exhibiton of the maps. Take turns to go around asking the map makers questions about what their maps show.

England - 1066

Before you go on holiday you might look at travel guides to find out what a place is like. When Duke William made up his mind to invade England in 1066 he must have had some idea about what the country was like, for he had visited it fifteen years earlier. My eleven-year-old daughter Eleanor used what historians tell us, to write the travel guide (**A**) about her imaginary trip to England in 1066.

A Norman monk, Orderic Vitalis (born c 1070) tells us in source **B** about Norman England. Orderic was brought up until the age of ten in Shrewsbury, where I used to live (which is why I wanted to find out about him). His mum and dad then sent him to Normandy to become a monk; we don't know why.

Orderic wrote the story of his life in Latin. A famous part of his book, source **B**, is one of a few written sources which give us clues about Norman England, which is why I have put it in. The Source has been translated from Latin into modern English:

> At this time (c 1070), by the grace of God peace reigned over England and its people could live happily. The English and Normans lived in peace side by side in towns and cities, and married each other. You could see many villages or town markets filled with displays of French goods… no one dared to pillage, but everyone farmed their own fields in safety and lived in peace with their neighbours. Churches were built and restored, and in them Holy men gave their lives to praying to God. Alas, this was not to last. (**B**)

(Orderic Vitalis c 1100 The Ecclesiastical History)

A

The weather is okay, in summer there are quite a few sunny days but it is also wet and cloudy. In winter there are some days of hard frost and snow, especially in the North. Spring is lovely, with lots of flowers. On land the Saxons travel mainly on foot along tracks or the old Roman roads, although they travel up big rivers and along the coast in boats, see map C. There are not many people living in England [only one-fiftieth of those today], about 1.25 million in all. Families are large, but most men and women are dead by the age of forty. People live mainly in thousands of villages and hamlets dotted across the country.

Most of the villages I passed through had peasant huts along each side of an earth street, which is a sea of mud in wet weather. At the end of the street was usually the hall of the local thane or lord and a small church. Outside the villages are large fields, where the peasants grow crops and raise animals.

There are a few small towns, really large villages with 2000 to 3000 people. Towns are widely spread out, see map D. To get to each town and village I passed through marshes, forests, heath and over grassy hills, and on the tracks met peasants and traders going to the town's market. Each town has its own wall or fence, to keep out enemies in time of war. I noticed workshops and a marketsquare in each town. The Saxons all worship Jesus Christ.

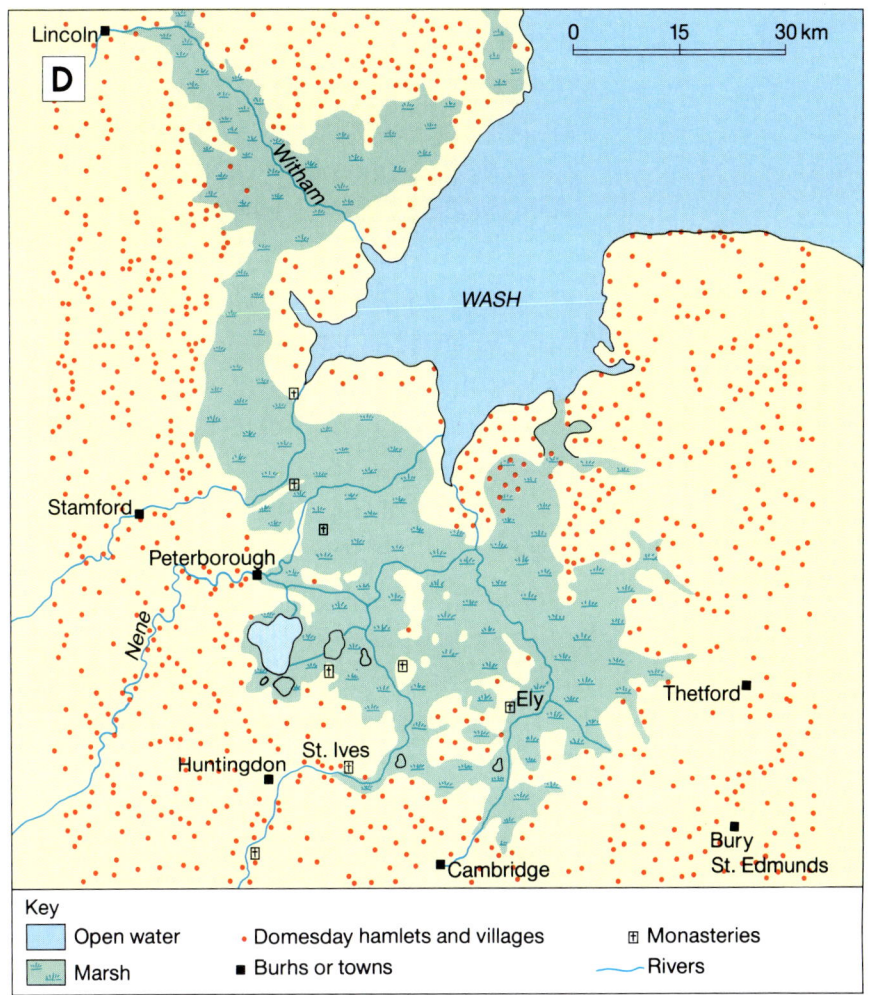

Travel Poster or Guide

You can use the facts and ideas you squeeze from sources **A-D** to help make up your own travel poster or guide to Norman England.

a Preparing your own travel poster (AT1).
To prepare your own travel poster or guide think of the things that you would mention. Here is a list you can add to: climate, countryside, travel, towns, villages, people, dress. Design your poster or guide so that it has clear, striking headlines and banners.

b Using the sources (AT3).
Work out the key things that you would like to put on the poster or guide. Look at each source in turn and think of the things you might take from it. Read through source **B**, and work out what each sentence means. How much trust can you place in source **B**?

Now finish the poster or guide, using what you have found out about Norman England to help you.

c Display (AT1).
You can hold a poster judging competition to see who has come up with the best poster for the class.

ACTIVITY

Who were the Normans?

If you had asked Alfred the Great (849-99), the great English King who beat the Vikings, about the Normans he would not have known what you were talking about. The reason is simple. The first Normans (= Norse men) only settled in northern France in 911. These Normans were a Viking band from Denmark. A local French ruler gave them land in return for fighting for him. The Viking settlers soon built up their own strong kingdom under their leader Rollo, the first Duke of Normandy. 150 years later their great-great-great-grandchildren invaded England with Duke William as their leader.

In THINKING HISTORY you build up your ideas as you go along, using your sources to help you. Sources **A-D** allow you to work out your own ideas about what these Normans were like. We provide a list of questions to which you can add your own. Asking questions is at the heart of THINKING HISTORY.

Quickly read accounts **A** and **B** - I picked them because they give two clear views of the Normans. On which points do they agree, and on which disagree? In trying to sort out our own ideas about the Normans we have to think hard about accounts like **A** and **B**. A Norman monk copied down **A**, which he claims records what William the Conqueror felt about his fellow Normans, while an Anglo-Saxon monk wrote **B**.

> *The Normans under a kind but firm ruler are a very brave race, braver than all others in facing danger and in trying to smash their enemies. But in peace they bring ruin by quarrelling among themselves. They are keen to rebel, being always ready to fight and ripe for crime. They must be kept in check by a strong, fair hand. Left alone they are like a wild, young, untamed colt let off the rein. Then their ruler faces ruin. I have learnt this from bitter experience. My nearest friends and my own family have plotted against me and tried to strip me of my family fortune. Instead, they should have helped me fight my enemies.* **(A)**

(William I, quoted by Orderic Vitalis c1100 *The Ecclesiastical History*)

> *The Normans were then [1066], as they are now, careful about how they dressed and careful about what they ate, but not too fussy. They are a race used to war and can hardly live without it. They attack their enemies with great force and when violence fails they use tricks or pay bribes. As I have said, they live cheaply in big houses, are jealous of their equals and try to get on equal terms with their betters. They strip their subjects of their wealth, although they protect them from others. They are faithful to their lords, but will betray them if at all upset. They are open to bribes and will betray their lords if they think they will win. They are the most polite of people and even marry their subjects. After they came to England they backed the church, which had become lifeless. You can see churches rise in every village, and they built monasteries in towns and cities in a style unknown to us.* **(B)**

(William of Malmesbury c 1125 *Gesta Regum Anglorum*)

C is a picture which contains clues about the Normans. The figure sitting in the clouds is meant to be God. What does this tell you about why the Normans fought so much? The Normans, men, women and children, spread and settled across Europe, and set up kingdoms in the Middle East, **D**.

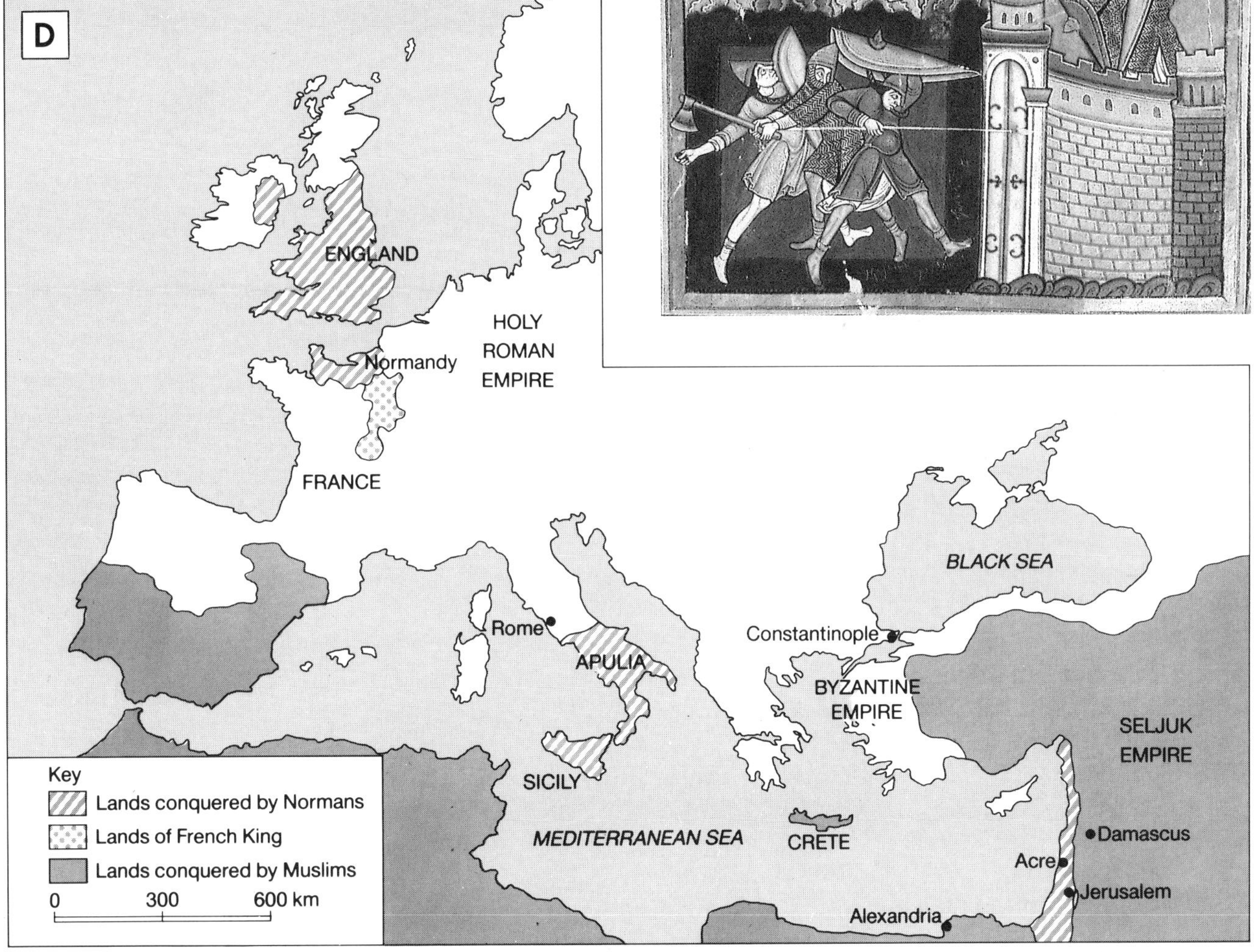

Thinking about the Normans - The Young Historian

To be an historian you first need to come up with some basic questions about the Normans. Then you have to think about how to find the answers.

a Asking questions (AT3). By yourself or in pairs put down three questions you can think of about the Normans. Examples are • Who were the Normans? • How did they fight? Then work out a class list - you can use this as the basis for the rest of your work.

b Finding answers (AT3). Look at the text and at sources **A**, **B**, **C** and **D**. What answers do these sources give to your questions?

c Can you trust the sources? (AT2). Why do you think Orderic (**A**) and William (**B**) say such different things about the Normans? Can they both be right?

d Star diagram (AT1). Use the ideas from tasks **b** and **c** to produce a star diagram about the Normans. Each point of the star will lead to one idea, such as 'where the Normans lived'. Build up the star as you go along, adding a new point for each new idea about the Normans.

e Using your imagination (AT1). What questions did you not find answers for? If you could interview William the Conqueror's ghost, what answers might he give to your questions?

Harold, William or Hardrada?

Think of the last time you had a row with someone. Did you both believe you were in the right even though you were quarrelling over the same facts? It is how you **interpret** (look at) the facts that matters. The fun of history often comes from trying to see who was right. That's if there *was* a right or wrong point of view!

We will look at the dispute over who should be King of England in 1066 from the points of view of the men who fought for the throne. They were Earl **Harold** of Wessex (see map **A**), **Harald Hardrada**, King of Norway, and **William**, Duke of Normandy. In THINKING HISTORY you have to try to see what men and women in the past thought and felt, and why they acted in a certain way.

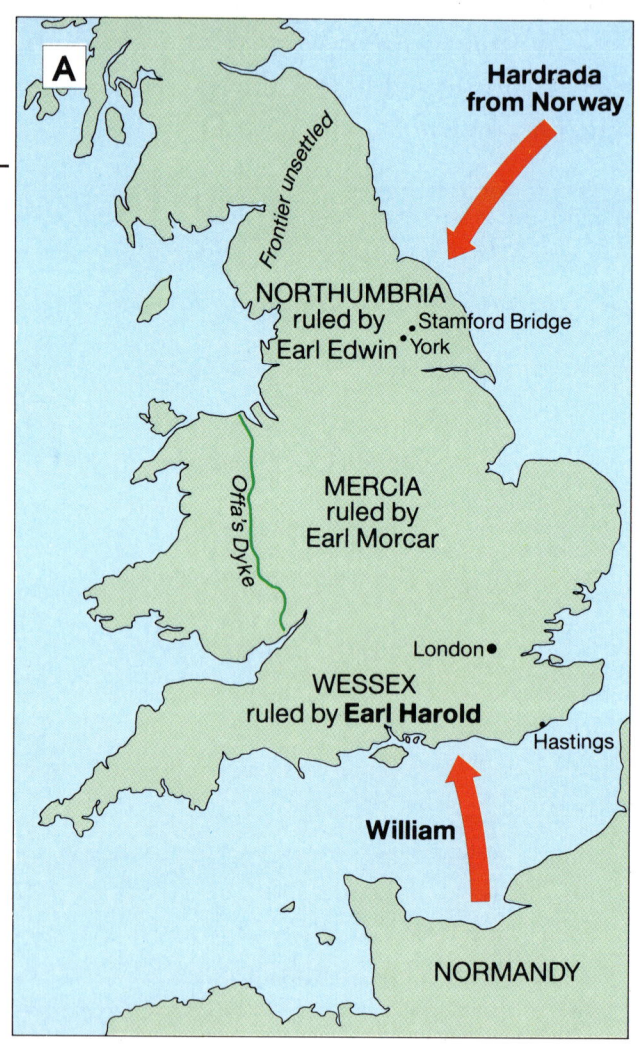

Court of Enquiry

Today courts sort out quarrels between people, and decide who is in the right or wrong. Set up a court to see who should have been England's new king in 1066. You are all members of the jury. Put forward your views as a report or part of a discussion. The court could even represent the Witan. Choose some class members to take the roles of Harold, William, Hardrada, the Pope and the Archbishop of Canterbury.

a Different viewpoints (AT2). Look at the claims of King Harold, Hardrada and Duke William from the viewpoints of ONE of the following. A backer of Harold OR William OR Hardrada; the Pope; the Archbishop of Canterbury. Copy the table below to judge Harold's, Hardrada's and William's claims from the viewpoint you have chosen. For each point put a ring around either S = Strong, F = Fair, W = Weak in the box in the table. You can do this by yourself or in pairs. Compare your table with the table produced from a different viewpoint.

WHOSE CLAIM?	THE KING'S HEIR	THE BACKING OF GOD
William's	Strong Fair Weak	Strong Fair Weak
Harold's	Strong Fair Weak	Strong Fair Weak
Hardrada's	Strong Fair Weak	Strong Fair Weak

b The court (AT2). Call each claimant to the throne, and ask them questions about their right to the throne. Call the Pope and the Archbishop of Canterbury, and ask them who they think should have the throne. Look with care at the evidence which they put forward.

c What do you think? (AT1) Produce a report on who you think has the best claim OR make a wall poster with the headline 'Long live King ....'

ACTIVITY · ACTIVITY

In 1066 a huge quarrel broke out over who should be King of England. The results of that quarrel still affect all our lives. It came into the open in January when King Edward the Confessor (1042-66) died. Edward had no heir old enough to be the strong king England needed. To advise him the English king had a great council (called the **Witan**) of leading nobles (called **thanes**). In January 1066 the Witan had to decide who should be the new king. What was the row about?

The King's Rightful Heir

a William said that the old King of England, Edward, had promised to make him the next king when William paid a visit to Edward's court in 1051.

b Harold of Wessex argued that King Edward named him as the next king of England at the end of his reign. The Witan also had the right to name the next king, and chose him.

c Hardrada was the heir of the Viking Kings of England (1016-42). A written treaty between the English and Danes seemed to back his claim to the English throne.

Hardrada argued that his claim was better than that of either Harold or William.

The Backing Of God

d William claimed that God was on his side. When Harold had visited Normandy in 1064 he had sworn an oath on Holy relics and the Bible, picture **B**, that he would back William's claim to be the next English king. The Pope had given William's claim his backing. The Pope also said that he had sacked the Archbishop of Canterbury. So the sacked Archbishop could not officially crown Earl Harold as king.

e In 1066 the Archbishop of Canterbury crowned Harold of Wessex in Westminster Abbey. Many people felt that this church service gave Harold the backing of God. Harold also said that Duke William's claim that God was on his side (see **d**) was false because William had forced Harold to swear a holy oath to back him. Harold was William's prisoner at the time.

f Hardrada argued that God had chosen him as Cnut's heir to take the English throne.

The Norman Invasion

History is made up of great stories, and one of the most exciting is of how Duke William invaded England. Men wrote down the story at the time it happened. Our best written account is the diary or chronicle of Duke William's own priest, William of Poitiers, **A**.

❝ *Duke William took counsel with his vassals and determined to avenge the wrong by arms and by arms to claim his inheritance, although many lords argued persuasively against the enterprise as too dangerous and far beyond the resources of Normandy.* ❞ (A)

This source is hard to understand. Look up the meaning of words you do not know. Then write out the passage in your own words.

Look at **B**. Who do you think the people in the picture are? What would it have been like to be there when the decision was taken to invade England? We can give the background facts in a simple **decision table**. I based the decision table on sources like William of Poitiers, and what they tell us were the choices which faced William in 1066. Use the choices you make from it to produce your own story book of the invasion.

Norman Conquest Adventure Story (AT1)

You can make up your own story or comic book about the Norman invasion, either as a simple tale or as a story which branches out along different lines, like an adventure book. But your story must be based on our sources, otherwise it will be a fairy story.

For your story:
• Decide on the role you would like to take. You could give your advice as a Norman knight, a priest or the son or daughter of one of his barons who sailed to England.
• Base your story on your choice at each point in the story- see the DECISION TABLE.
• You can write it as a diary or chronicle, or as a series of letters to your closest friend.

ACTIVITY · ACTIVITY ·

DECISION TABLE

CHOOSE ONE DECISION AT EACH POINT

Decision One. February 1066. You are one of William's Council **(B)**, advising him on whether to invade England or not. One problem is that his neighbours could invade Normandy, **(D)**. Conan of Brittany is an old enemy. He might seize the chance of William being in England to grab lands on the borders of Normandy. Look at **D**. Why are there so many castles? What does this suggest about the problems William might face if he sails abroad?

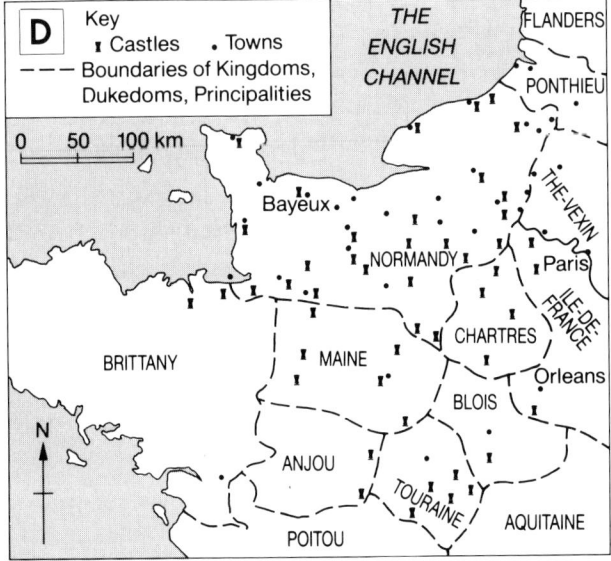

You can talk with your wife about what you would advise William to do. Should he:

1 Ally with Hardrada to jointly invade England? They could then split the country up between them. OR
2 Ally with Edwin and Morcar (see page 10 **A**)? They would keep their own earldoms while William would have the earldom of King Harold OR
3 Go it alone? OR
4 Do one of **1-3**, and make a treaty with local Norman lords? Use **D** to work out how many neighbours he will have to make a treaty with. He could pay them to be quiet, or promise them lands in England in return for support. They might even send archers, footsoldiers and knights to England with William. OR
5 Another plan?

Decision Two. May 1066. William pushes on with building boats for the invasion **(C)**. What do you think **C** suggests about the problems he faced in building a fleet, and how long it might take? William will need as many good fighting men as he can raise. As a member of William's council, after talking to your wife would you advise him to:

6 Only take Norman soldiers with him from Normandy? OR
7 Get more troops from the rest of France? This will take time. This might mean it will be too late in the year to invade England, autumn storms could easily wreck his fleet, and it is hard to fight in the cold, rain, slush and mud of an English winter OR
8 Try another plan?

Decision Three. June 1066. What kind of troops would you advise William to take with him? Having talked the decision over with your wife, would you advise William to:

9 Rely only on footsoldiers to fight the 2000 housecarls of Harold? Harold's Saxon nobles or thanes fight on foot with battle axes, swords and spears, and wear helmets and chain mail OR
10 Bring his Norman war horses with him? It would be hard to take them on the boats. Can you think why? The boats were made out of wooden planks, open to the sea and about as long as a classroom. Think of a horse breaking loose in a ship, wild with anger, hooves flying... But horses would make a great difference in battle. They can strike terror into the enemies' hearts OR
11 Try another plan?

Decision Four. October 1066. Winds blowing in from the channel have kept William in harbour - his fleet is built, and the troops are raring to go. News has arrived that King Harold has marched North to fight Hardrada of Norway, who has landed with an army. Would you advise William to:

12 Sail for London? OR
13 Sail to the nearest point on the South coast? OR
14 Sail to Northumbria, where King Harold cannot rely on the backing of Earl Morcar? OR
15 Try another plan?

At last William managed to get out of port, with his ships loaded down food, weapons, men and horses.

The Battle of Hastings

"Smashing victory - Norman triumph" or "England's darkest hour" - read all about it! If there had been newspapers in 1066, these could have been their headlines. The newsflashes, pictures and maps below are the kind of evidence that is used to write newspapers. I made up the newsflashes, using a pile of History books to sort out facts and ideas.

A (map showing):
- Hardrada's route
- ③ Tostig joins Harold Hardrada from Norway. They attack NE coast with combined fleet of 300 ships
- ⑤ 25 Sept Battle of Stamford Bridge. Tostig and Hardrada defeated and killed
- ④ 20 Sept Battle of Fulford. Edwin defeated
- York
- ② June Earl Edwin of Mercia defeats Tostig
- King Harold's movements
- ENGLAND
- ⑧ 25 Dec William crowned King of England — Berkhamsted, London
- ⑦ 14 Oct 1066 Battle of Hastings. Harold killed
- Kent
- ⑥ 27,28 Sept William sails for England
- ISLE OF WIGHT
- ① Tostig (Harold's brother) raids Isle of Wight and Kent, then continues north
- ENGLISH CHANNEL
- St. Valéry
- Normandy
- NORTH SEA

NEWSFLASH (1)

September 20, Fulford. Hardrada defeats Edwin and Morcar... Harold is racing north to York with his bodyguard... Harold's soldiers join up with the surviving housecarls and thanes of Edwin and Morcar... **September 25, Stamford Bridge.** It is now known that Harold's brother Tostig is with Hardrada... Hardrada and Tostig caught in surprise attack by Harold (map **A**)... bloody, hard fought battle... Evening: Tostig and Hardrada lie dead on the battlefield here at Stamford Bridge... Hardrada came to Northumberland with some 300 ships, only 24 carried away the survivors... News has come that Duke William's army has landed on the south coast... Harold's army is riding off to the south at great speed.

NEWSFLASH (2)

October 14, Hastings. Harold has drawn up his line of housecarls (his highly-trained professional soldiers) behind their shields on the crest of a hill, (plan **B**)... In front and on his flank are his lightly armed footsoldiers, the fyrd (peasant army)... Facing Harold is William's force of archers and footsoldiers... there seem to be around 2,000 knights mounted on horseback, sitting behind William's footsoldiers (**C**). William's archers shower the Anglo-Saxon line with arrows, then William and his knights charge up the hill to try to hack through the Anglo-Saxon line... William has led many charges but they have all failed...William appears to be retreating...great cheers from Harold's fyrd ... the fyrd has broken its line and is chasing down towards the retreating Normans... terrible slaughter... William's army has suddenly turned on the little groups of Harold's soldiers... now that their line is broken up the Anglo-Saxons are being hacked to pieces (**D**)... William's cavalry have battered through the housecarls' wall of shields,... Harold and his two brothers have been killed (see page 2)... William now has England at his mercy.

NEWSFLASH (3).

December 20, London Reports flooding in of the terror and destruction Duke William has caused... his army has robbed and killed everyone in its way... villages left burnt to the ground... judging from the reports, William's march from Hastings to London took a round-about route (see map **A**)... the Anglo-Saxon leaders have no wish to fight on...
December 25, Westminster Abbey. The English Earls and Bishops have gathered to greet William... Duke William crowns himself King of England.

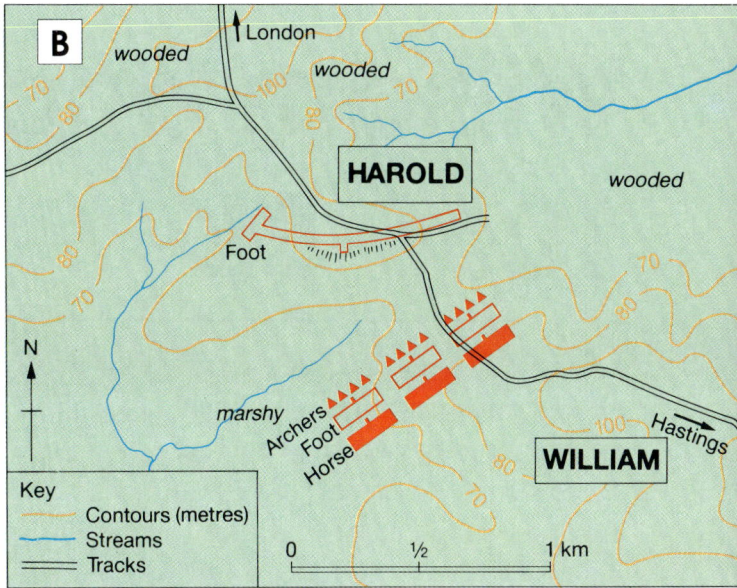

Read all about it!

You can use the newsflashes, maps and pictures to prepare your own newspapers about the Battle of Hastings.

a Whose side are you on? (AT2). You have to edit and write the story of The Battle of Hastings from the viewpoint of either The Norman Times of Duke William or The Anglo-Saxon Chronicle of King Harold or The Viking Saga of Hardrada. Choose ONE of these newspapers. Take each newsflash in turn, and by yourself or in groups prepare:

1 Headlines. In turn, for each set of newsflashes, produce a headline or headlines with the main story line you want to put across. The headlines should tell what happened from the point of view of your newspaper, ie Harold's, William's, or Hardrada's point of view.

2 The main story. An account of what is going on, again writing it from the viewpoint of your newspaper. You can tell the story in the form of a chart or a set of drawings, like a picture story in a comic.

3 Comment. What do you feel about events, from the viewpoint of the editor of the newspaper. You can also comment on what might happen in the future. For example, after the Battle of Hastings you can say what you think William might do and what kind of ruler he might be.

4 Cartoons and drawings. Cartoons must be based on the facts as you know them, and highlight what is going on.

5 Timeline. Timeline of events in the newsflash.

6 Maps - battle plans as needed.

b Read all about it? (AT2). Compare the stories from each newspaper and discuss how and why they differ. Put up your newspapers as a wall display.

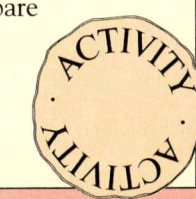

William and England, 1066-86

History is like an adventure book where almost **anything might happen next**. How might things have turned out after the Battle of Hastings? Although William had been crowned King of England, his army of 2000 cavalry and some 5000 footsoldiers only ruled as far as they could see. William had to cope with many threats. In France he had to make sure Normandy's strong neighbours did not attack his dukedom. In England there was a constant danger of Viking invasions from Denmark and Norway, and the Saxon earls and thanes were always ready to revolt against him.

Imagine you are a member of William's Council in 1067. You are giving him advice on what to do when faced with these problems.

> **Decision One.** In 1067 should William:
>
> **1** Keep Edwin and Morcar as rulers of Mercia and Northumbria with their thanes, and give his followers the lands of Harold and his family? OR
> **2** Remove all the Saxon earls and thanes and hand their lands over to his Norman followers? OR
> **3** Make the Saxon earls live at court as his hostages and build castles throughout England? Castles were how a handful of Norman soldiers could keep a grip on the villages around them (see page 18).

William had every reason to be afraid. In 1067 he crushed a rising in the West of England after he had besieged the town of Exeter for 18 days. 1069 saw the greatest threat to William, the northern rising. I chose **A**, an extract from the Anglo-Saxon Chronicle, because it tells the story in a vivid and clear way:

> *Soon thereafter three sons of King Swein with two hundred and forty ships came from Denmark into the Humber. There they were met by Prince Edgar, Earl Waltheof, Maerleswein and Earl Gospatric with the Northumbrians and all the people of the country. Forming an immense army, riding and marching in high spirits, they all marched on York and stormed and destroyed the castle. They seized countless treasures in it, slayed many hundreds of French men and carried off great numbers to their ships.* **(A)**

(The Anglo-Saxon Chronicle, 1069)

> **Decision Two.** Should William:
>
> **4** Make peace with Swein's sons, Prince Edgar and Earl Waltheof? OR
> **5** March north with an army, defeat the invaders and treat the people with kindness? OR
> **6** March north with an army, destroy everything in his path, defeat the invaders and kill them all?

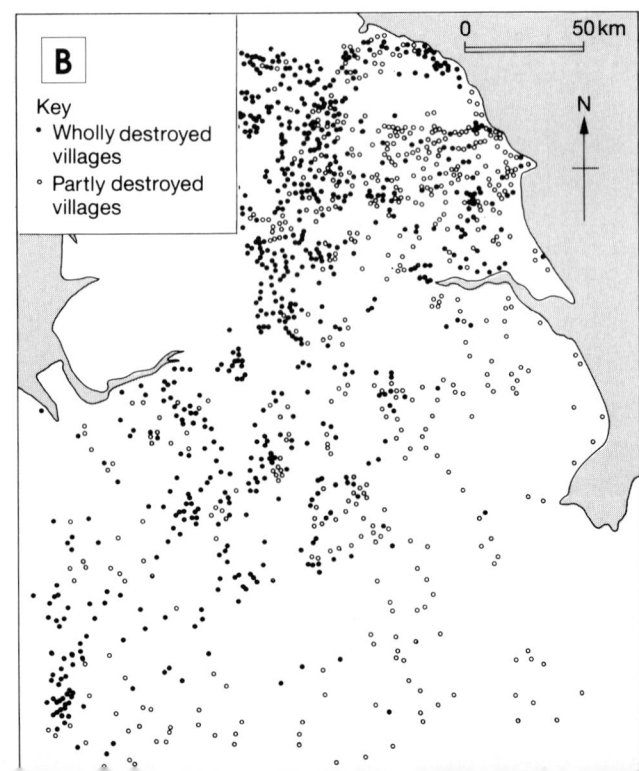

B
Key
• Wholly destroyed villages
◦ Partly destroyed villages

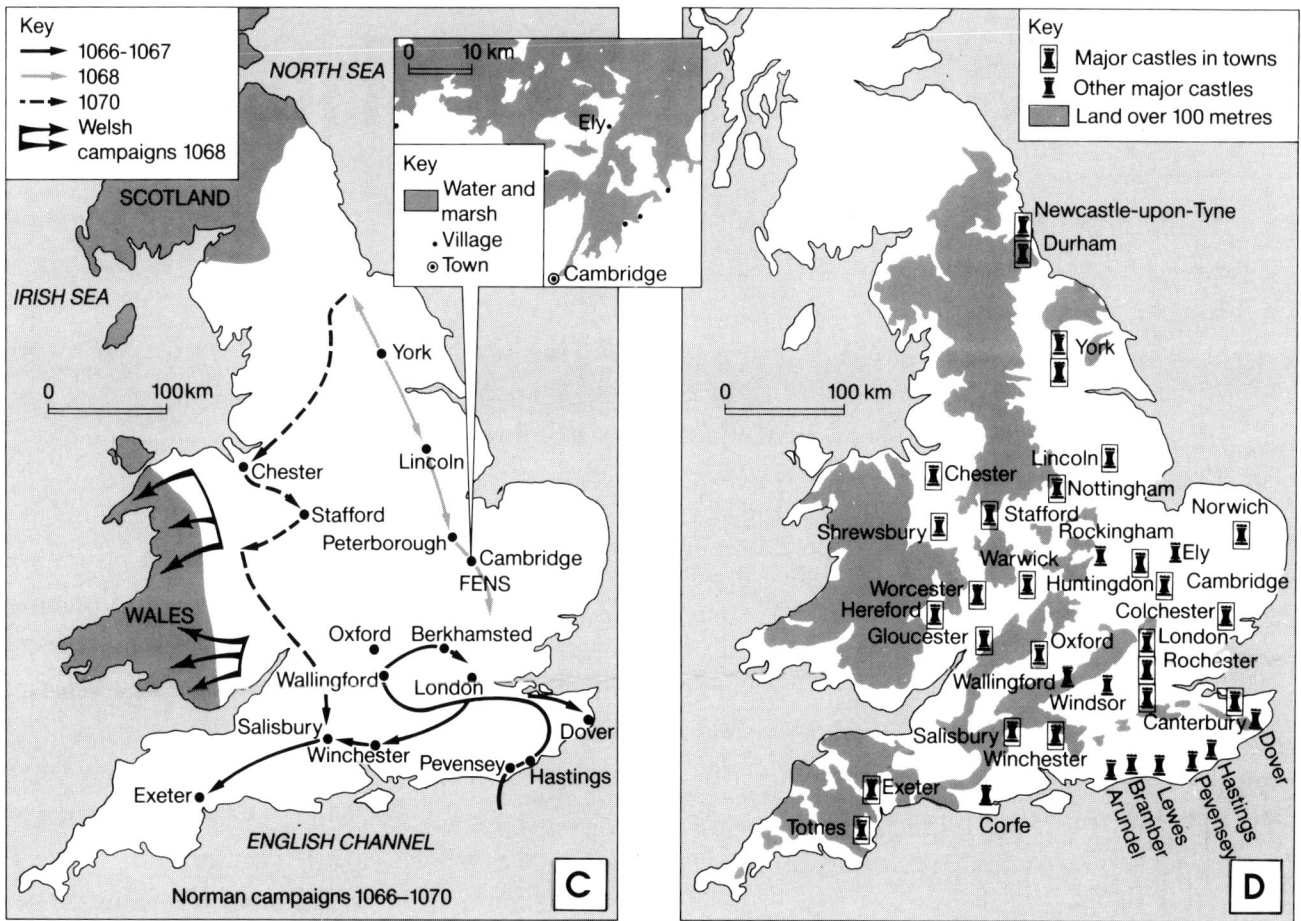

Norman campaigns 1066–1070

B suggests what William actually did. From 1070-71 William struggled against the revolt of Hereward the Wake in the fens of East Anglia, C. Hereward fought alongside earls Edwin and Morcar who had risen against William, and a Danish army.

Decision Three. Should William:

7 Pay the Danes to go home and then attack the rebels' base at Ely? OR
8 At once use a fleet of small boats to attack Ely? OR
9 Make peace with Edwin and Morcar and then attack Hereward and the Danes?

By 1071 the rising of Hereward had been put down, the Danes, Edwin and Morcar were defeated. No one knows what happened to Hereward but his name lives on as a symbol of heroic struggle against an invader. By 1080 William had split up the land of England among his followers, who built castles wherever they settled (**D**).

William and England - Adventure Story, 1066-1080

When you create an adventure story or book, you must make sure that you are clear about the background events.

a Timeline (AT1). Read through this chapter and put the main events on to a timeline for 1066-1080.
b The Norman Settlement (AT1). By yourself or in pairs, work out the plans you would have recommended William to follow.
c Class decision (AT1). You can now pool your ideas, and come to a class decision. ONLY THEN look at the decisions William actually took, at the bottom of this box.
d Story book (AT1, AT3). Record your ideas in the form of a story or adventure book, or put them on a map, or make a picture story with captions. In your story book mention what you can work out from maps **B-D**. How much killing, burning and plundering does **B** suggest? What problems faced William in fighting Hereward (**C**)? What does **D** suggest about the role which castles played in keeping the English down?

William's decisions: 1, 6, 8.

Castles and Knights

King William split up England between his lords, like Judhael of Totnes, who had fought for him. In turn, Judhael split up his land between his knights (see page 22). Often the knight's wife would take over the knight's jobs when he was at war or if he died. Can you think what problems a knight and his wife would face when they took over the villages their lord had granted them?

Imagine you are a Norman knight or his wife. To keep the native Anglo-Saxons under your thumb you would have to build a castle in your main village like the one William had put up at Hastings when he landed, (**A**). The area you rule has no roads, only dirt tracks and the countryside is covered in forest. Where would you put your castle? To learn about the **sites** of Norman castles, I used my own county, Shropshire, which has a lot of Norman **Motte and Bailey** castles. Shropshire is a county on the English-Welsh border. Norman knights seem to have chosen sites for castles which had the following features.

1 They were in a position to stop bands of enemy raiders from using tracks to the main town in an area.
2 They were on the edge of high land, or in the middle of a group of villages.
3 They were a half a day's march from each other - from 5 to 10 kilometres.

The Normans also built one main castle in the area's chief town. What did a Norman castle look like? **B** is a famous artist's drawing of a typical Motte and Bailey. The Motte (mound) is the tower. The Bailey (enclosure) is the courtyard where the knight and his soldiers lived, and where peasants and their animals fled to safety in times of war. I always use this artist's drawings because they bring the past to life in a real way. He took great care to get his facts right. Can you think what the artist based his drawing on?

Motte and Bailey castles had many shapes. **C** is a plan of Hen Domen, on the Welsh borders. I know about it because the archaeologist who excavated it taught me at school.

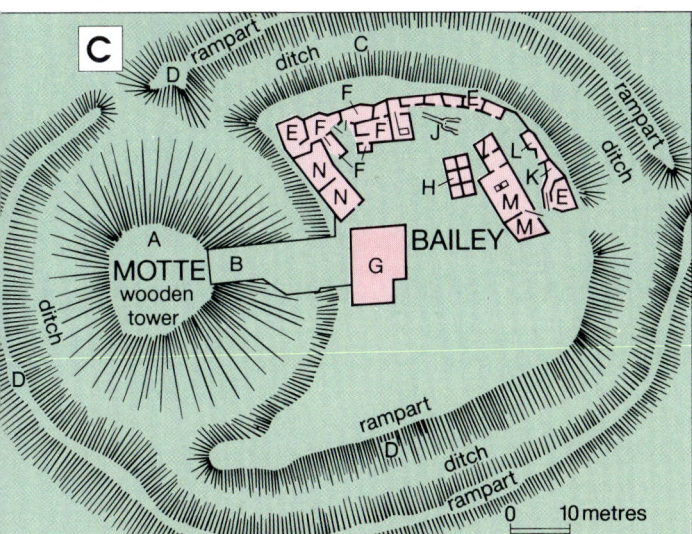

Key
A A wooden tower, with a high fence around it
B A drawbridge from the Motte to the Bailey
C A ditch around both the Motte and the Bailey
D A high fence around the Bailey
E Fighting platforms/towers at the corner of the Bailey
F Huts for the men to live in
G Stables for the horses
H A granary
I A cookhouse
J A well, with rain pipes from the hut roofs
K A guardroom at the entrance to the Bailey
L A weapons store
M A hall where the troops could meet, and which was the home of the Knight in time of war
N A small chapel

The Norman Castle

How well would you solve the problems which faced a Norman Knight? Choose one of the tasks. When you have solved your problem, get together with the rest of the class to share your ideas.

a Getting Anglo-Saxons to understand you (AT1).
• You cannot speak their language. Think of what it would be like to go abroad and not speak a word of the local language, nor be able to read a word of it. The natives do not speak English.
• Work out ways to pass a message without speaking or writing. Try mime or drawing pictures!

b Controlling your local area (AT1, AT3).
• Look at a map of the area ten kilometres around your school. Mark the rivers, high and low land, and where small villages might have been in Norman times.
• Then work out where you think the Norman lord and his knights might have built their castles.

c Planning a Motte and Bailey Castle (AT1, AT3).
• Work out what each of the features shown in C was used for. How accurate is C likely to be?
• See which of these features you can see in B. What do you think B is based on? Can you trust it?
• Draw a map of the area on which your school stands. Show the main features, ie high land and streams.
• Taking this map, plan out your own Motte and Bailey castle. Include all the features you can see on B and C. Work out how you would have built it using local villagers to help you.
• Draw your castle, or make a cut out model to the scale of the features shown on Source C.
• Think of how you might have attacked or defended a Motte and Bailey castle.

ACTIVITY · ACTIVITY

Domesday Book

A brown envelope thuds through the letter box. Oh no ! My income tax form. Today the government has to find out about what we earn in order to raise taxes. In 1085 King William was faced with the same problem. He didn't know who owned what land, or how much tax he should get in. He also knew that he might need to spend much more money next year. William had learned that King Cnut of Denmark was about to invade England, so William had raised a large army to fight him. Although Cnut did not in fact come, William kept half his army at the ready, which cost a lot of money.

So William and his council gave orders for a survey of the whole of England, the Domesday Survey. William split the country up into seven areas. Our only source for what he decided is what the Anglo-Saxon Chronicle tells us :

> *Then he sent his men all over England into every shire to find out how many hundreds of 'hides' of land there were in each shire, and how much land and live-stock the king himself owned in the country, and what annual sums were lawfully his from each shire. He also had it recorded how much land his archbishops had and his bishops, his abbots and his earls, and - though I may be going into too great detail - how much each man who was a landholder here in England had in land or in live-stock, and how much money it was worth. So very thoroughly did he have the inquiry carried out that there was not a single 'hide' not one virgate of land, not even - it is shameful to record it, but it did not seem shameful to him to do - not even one ox, nor one cow, nor one pig which escaped notice in his survey.* **(A)**

(The Anglo-Saxon Chronicle)

FACTFILE

> *HOLY TRINITY ABBEY, ROUEN **(1)** holds **HERMONDESWORDE (2)** from the King. It answers for 30 hides. **(3)** Land for 20 ploughs **(4)**. 8 hides belong to the Lordship; 3 ploughs there. There are 10 ploughs between the Frenchmen **(5)** and the villagers; a further 7 ploughs possible. A man at arms **(6)** has 2 hides; 2 villagers, 1 hide each: 2 villagers with 1 hide; 14 villagers with 1 virgate **(7)** each; 6 villagers with 1/2 virgate each, 6 smallholders **(8)**, 5 acres each; 7 cottages **(9)**; 6 slaves **(10)**: 3 mills at 60 shillings and 500 eels **(11)**: from the fishponds 1000 eels; meadow got 20 ploughs; pasture for village livestock; woodland, 500 pigs **(12)**; 1 arpent of vines **(13)**. Total value **(14)** £20: when acquired £12; in the time of King Edward £25. Earl Harold held this manor **(15)**. In this manor there was a Freeman **(16)** who held 2 of those 30 hides: in the time of King Edward he could not grant or sell this land out-side Hermondesworde.* **(B)**

Some notes to help you understand the entry for Harmondsworth.
(1) The manor of Harmondsworth was granted to a French monastery in Rouen.
(2) The place name has changed.
(3) A hide was an amount of land perhaps 120 acres.
(4) An area of land requiring 20 teams of oxen to plough it.
(5) Settlers from France who have arrived since the Conquest.
(6) A man who had to give military service for his land.
(7) A virgate was a quarter of a hide.
(8) Smallholders were middle class peasants.
(9) A cottager owned a house but little or no land.
(10) Slaves had to work for other people and could not and were not free to do anything without permission.
(11) Rent for the water-mill was paid in money and eels!
(12) Enough woodland for 500 pigs to find food (acorns) in.
(13) An arpent was an acre.
(14) The total income of the manor is given for three dates.
(15) This is Harold who was killed at the Battle of Hastings.
(16) A Freeman and independent peasant, of higher class than the other villagers . But he wasn't free to sell his land to anybody outside the manor.

Why do you think that the writer of the Anglo-Saxon Chronicle felt that William's survey was shameful? The answers to all the questions were sorted out and written down in the Domesday Book, **B**. If you live in England, you should be able to look up your local Domesday Book entries. The Fact file shows the entry for Harmondsworth, Middlesex.

A Domesday entry for a place called Wyke near where I live really excited me, because we wrote a place-names computer program, and Wyke means dairy farm. In the Domesday Book it lists the animals which lived there - the dairy farm came to life! Working out what Domesday entries mean can be great fun.

Domesday Tax Survey

When we fill in government tax forms we have to look at the evidence which we have about how much we earn and spend and how many people live in our home, just like the Domesday enquiry. How would you cope with a Domesday Tax survey today?

a Studying the Sources (AT2, AT3).
1 In History we use our sources to find things out. Source work can be very hard. **A** is a key source; I chose it because it helps us see what happened in 1086. Read **A** with great care. Look up the meaning of any words that you do not know.
2 What idea does the extract give of what the Domesday survey was like?
3 What clues does it contain as to what the writer felt about it?
4 What impression does it give of King William?
5 Think of how you might feel if you had to go and give evidence to William's Domesday commissioners.

b Domesday Survey (AT1). Look out of the window.
• Pretend that we have travelled back to 1087, and that you are a peasant living in a local village (see page 56).
• A stranger rides down a dusty track to the village **C**.
• The knight's reeve or steward, who runs the village for him, calls the villagers together that evening in the parish church. • He says the stranger has told him to go with the priest and six peasants to tell King William's men what the village is worth.
• You go with the reeve to the local town and answer these questions:

The Commissioners' Questions

What is the manor called?
Who held it in the time of King Edward (20 years ago)?
Who holds it now?
How many acres?
How many ploughs?
How many acres does the lord own?
How many villeins (rich peasants)?
How many bordars (well off peasants)?
How many cottars (poor peasants)?
How many slaves?
How much wood?
How much meadow?
How much pasture?
How many sheep?
How many swine?
How many horses?
How many goats?
How many mills?
How many fish ponds?

c Map (AT1). Draw a map of your village using your answers. You could use graph paper, and mark four squares for a hide, one for a virgate.
d Local Domesday (AT3). If you have the actual Domesday entry for your area, follow these steps.
• Use **B** to work out what your entry means.
• Plan out how the village might have appeared then.
e Display (AT1). Put up your maps and plans as a wall display.

The Feudal System

Kings and Queens, Bishops and Knights, Castles and Peasants (Pawns) are all pieces in a modern game, **A**. Do you know which one? The game is based on how medieval society worked. Medieval kings had a huge problem. How could they rule the country peacefully and raise an army when they needed one without raising heavy taxes and spending loads of money?

The answer they came up with is what we call the feudal system. The King owned all the land, and lent it to his tenants-in-chief in return for a promise or oath that they would fight for him when he asked, **B**. Taking the oath was called doing homage. The king's tenants in turn would lend their land to knights who would fight for them when asked. The knights split up the land of their villages or manors among their peasants. They would protect the peasants from attack, and run the local court to enforce the law and sort out quarrels between them. In return the peasants worked for the local lord on his lands or demesne.

Medieval society can be seen as a sort of pyramid (**C**). But to think of medieval society as a *neat* pyramid is wrong. The whole thing was an awful muddle, with bishops, barons, earls and knights taking oaths to each other all over the place. The scope for quarrels was huge. What happened if two lords to whom you had sworn homage for different villages were fighting each other! They could both insist that you fight for them. What would you do?

Reliving the Feudal System

A good way to get to grips with the Feudal system is to plan a classroom drama.

a Social pyramids - paying homage today (AT2).
1 A headteacher, deputies and teachers run your school and tell the pupils what to do. Draw a feudal pyramid like **C** to show how your school works and the links between those who work in it.
2 Work out a charter or contract between you and your school. What does the school promise to do for you? What do you promise to do in return?
3 Work out the roles of the chessmen in **A**. You can do this from the names for the pieces. Draw these as feudal pyramid.

b Paying homage - the Middle Ages (AT3, AT1).
1 How would you pay homage? As a form you can act this out. Remember that women can serve as tenants-in-chief and under-tenants. The teacher is the local lord (tenant-in-chief) and s/he can choose two form members to be witnesses, the local bishop and his chief knight. First of all study **B** to work out what is going on in the picture. What is each person doing?
2 You are going to swear homage for the hut you live in and the land you farm. Write down its name on a piece of a paper, and what service you will do to your lord in return for your holding.
3 Bargain with your lord and his witnesses to see what terms they will give you for your holding. When you have agreed on these terms, swear homage (make your promise) as shown in **B**.
4 Make out a charter which shows that you hold your land, the service that you will do your lord and the protection that he will give you.

ACTIVITY

C

THE KING OWNS ALL THE LAND

The king keeps some land, about a quarter.
The rest he hands out to his tenants-in-chief, barons and bishops.

The king keeps the peace, judges cases and protects his tenants-in-chief from their enemies.

TENANTS-IN-CHIEF ABOUT 200

The tenants-in-chief keep some land, their manors, and hand the rest to their under-tenants. The under-tenants are mainly knights, lords and ladies.

The tenants-in-chief fight for the king when asked, and carry out other duties like serving as judges.

UNDER-TENANTS ABOUT 1000

The under-tenants keep some land, the demesne, in their manors and hand the rest over to the peasants to farm.

The under-tenants fight for his/her tenant-in-chief when asked and carry out duties like castle guard.

PEASANTS 1-1.25 million

The under-tenant protects the peasants from attack and gives out justice in the manor-court.

The peasants (see pages 58-63) work for the under-tenant on the demesne farm and pay fines for their land in the manor court (see pages 64-65).

Death in the Cathedral

The body lay lifeless on the floor. Fragments of its skull and brains were spattered over the steps. The corpse was that of Becket, Archbishop of Canterbury, and he lay dead near the altar of his own cathedral, **A**. One way to find out about his death is to investigate it as if you were writing a radio programme on how he died. What questions can you think of straight away?

Source **B** fills in the background. I wrote it, using a university textbook to help me.

❝*In 1162 Henry II, King of England, made his chief minister, who was also his best friend and drinking mate, Thomas Becket, Archbishop of Canterbury. Here was the chance to get the church back under control, a church with a vast amount of land and wealth, for it owned about a quarter of the land in England. Henry's plans turned sour, because Archbishop Becket became a devout Christian and stood up for the bishops and priests against the King. The King was furious, and in 1164 Becket fled abroad. For six years the row between Henry and Becket raged, and came to a head in 1170. Henry had his son crowned in June as England's next king against the express orders of Becket. Becket, as Archbishop of Canterbury, was the only person who could officially crown Henry's son. In December Becket came back to England to patch up the quarrel but Henry was still mad with anger. Four knights were sure that the King wanted Becket to be sorted out, so on 29 December they rode hell for leather to Canterbury to murder Becket.*❞ **(B)**

C is a medieval strip cartoon of how Becket died. The picture was drawn ten years after Becket died. It shows the four knights arriving at the cathedral. Can you see what

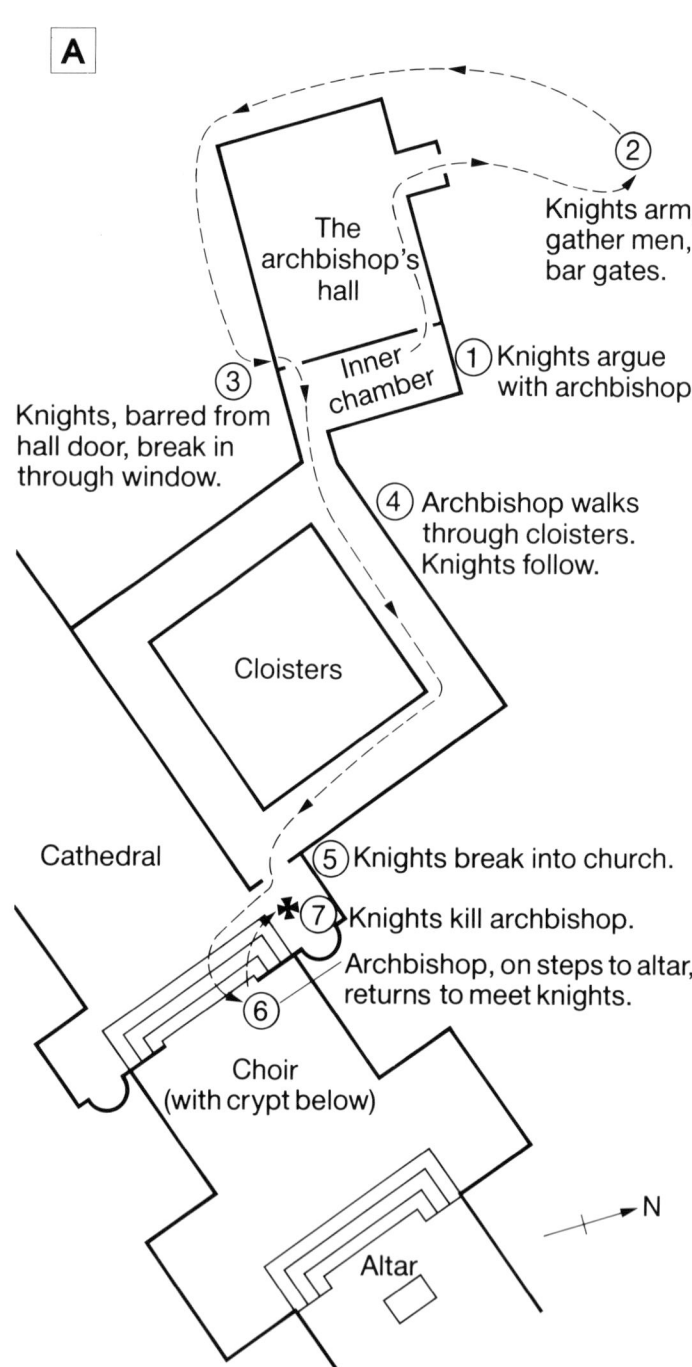

happened next? Edward Grim, a monk, wrote **D** and was with Becket when he died. I picked **D** because it is the most vivid account of the killing, and chose from it what I think are the key parts. The full document is at least five times as long. Can you already say what caused Becket's death?

24

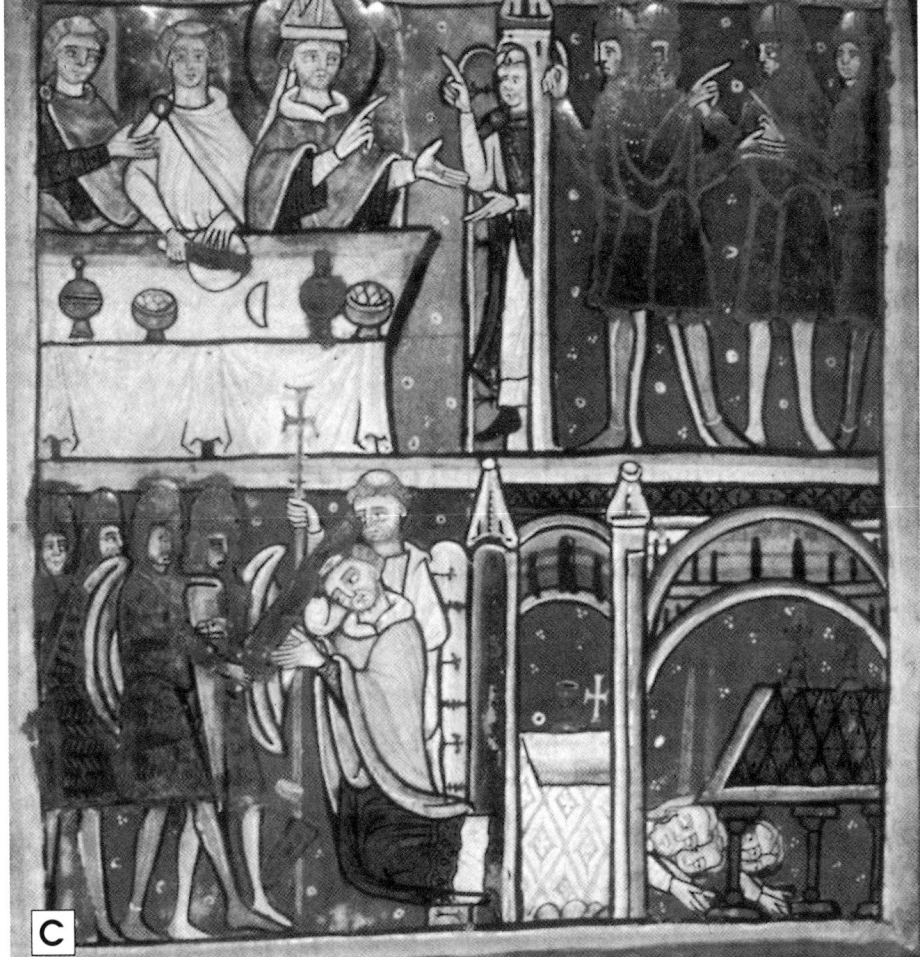

(C)

❝ The murderers cried, "you shall die at once and get what is coming to you". He replied, "I too am ready to die for my Lord, that in my blood the Church may obtain peace and freedom…"

Then they rushed at him and laid ungodly hands on him. The knights tried to get him outside the walls of the church there to slay him, or bind him and carry him off prisoner, as they later said was their plan. But as he could not easily be moved from the pillar, one of them seized hold of him and clung to him more closely. [Becket realises he is about to die.] Bending his head as if in prayer and joining his hands together and lifting them up, he left his cause in the hands of God and St Mary and the blessed martyr St Dennis. Scarce had he said these words than the wicked knight, fearing lest the people would rescue Becket and he would escape alive, leapt suddenly upon him and wounded the sacrificial lamb of God in the head cutting off the top of the crown… and by the same stroke he almost cut off the arm of him who tells the story.

Next Becket received a second blow on the head, but he still stood firm and unmoved. At the third blow he fell on his knees and elbows, offering himself a living sacrifice and saying in a low voice, "For the Name of Jesus and to protect the Church I am ready to embrace death." But the third knight struck an awful blow as he lay full length. The crown of Becket's head, which was large, was split away from the head in such a way that the blood, white with the brain and the brain, no less red from the blood, dyed the floor of the cathedral with the white of the lily and the red of the rose. **❞** (D)

(Edward Grim)

The History Programme

a Preliminary enquiry (AT3).
- Who is the body?
- How was Becket killed?
- How many people killed him?
- What weapons were used?
- Who were the witnesses?
- Where was Becket killed?
- Who killed him?
- Why was Becket killed?

b How reliable are the sources? (AT3).
- Can you believe what **B** tells you? Why/why not?
- Does **C** give an accurate idea of what went on?
- In **D** are there any clues which tell us that it is a true account? Is it likely to be exaggerated? Is it biased?
- What other things do the sources tell you about the murder?

c Sorting out your ideas (AT1).
- Say what is the background to the murder.
- Give the reasons for Becket being killed.
- Describe the scene of the murder.
- Draw a picture of the scene, or a cartoon showing what happened.
- Pick out who were the guilty, and suggest how they should be treated.

d The programme (AT1).
Have a narrator, who sets the scene and carries on the story. Work out parts for the people who were involved in the murder, and write scenes for them:
- Henry II
- Becket
- Edward Grim
- The four Knights
- The priests in the cathedral.

Henry II, 1154-89

When our Queen Elizabeth II dies, the papers will tell the story of her life in an **obituary**. What kind of obituary would you write for Henry II, King of England, given the clues in sources **A-D**? Map **A** shows the lands Henry ruled in France as well as England. **B**, drawn over 200 years later, shows Henry having a furious row with his Archbishop of Canterbury, Thomas Becket - see pages 24-25.

The writer Gerald of Wales gives us a gripping view of Henry in his chronicle (**C**). It always strikes me as the best eyewitness account we have of Henry. Chart **D** outlines how Henry and other medieval kings ran their affairs. I put it in so you can work out how he ruled.

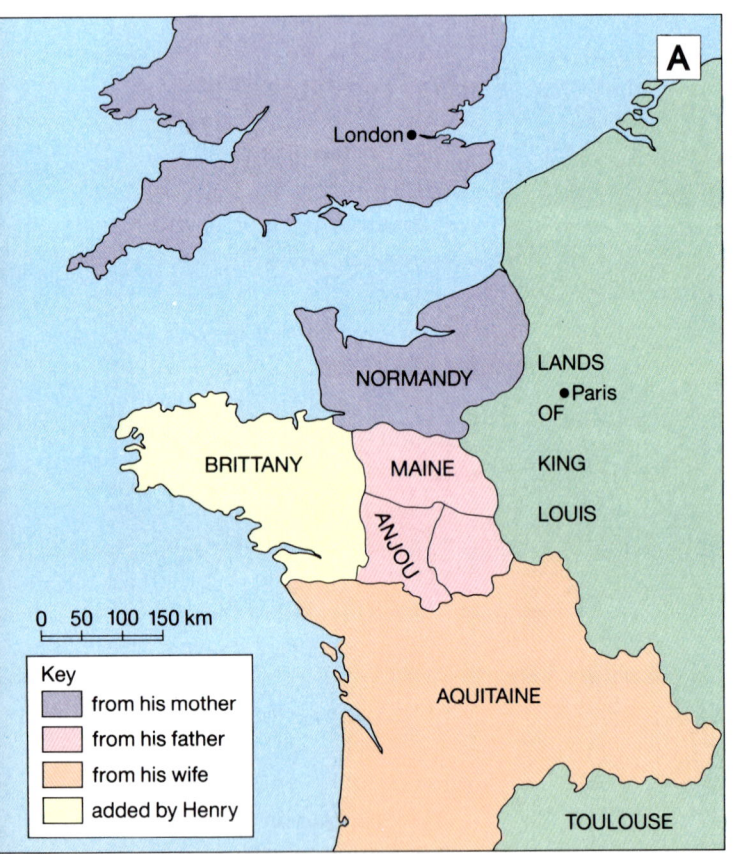

66 *Henry II, King of England, had a red, freckled face with a large, round head, grey eyes which glowed brightly and grew bloodshot when he was angry, a fierce look and a harsh, cracked voice. His neck thrust forward a bit from his shoulders, he had a broad, square chest and thick strong arms. With his squat frame he tended to run to fat, not from over eating for he took a lot of exercise but because of his build. He drank and ate as much as he needed...*

In times of war, which often threatened, he had little time to spare for running the government, and in times of peace he was never still nor resting. He was keen on hunting beyond belief, at the crack of dawn he was off on horseback, riding across waste land, deep into forests and climbing mountains... On his return he was rarely seen to sit down either before or after supper, which wore out his nobles.

He took great care to keep the peace, was very generous in giving alms to the poor and a great defender of the Holy Land. A lover of humility, he put down the nobles and sent the rich away empty handed.

To keep a grip on his kingdom Henry travelled non-stop from one province to the next. Because of his fierce temper and the rows he had, he quarreled with his wife Eleanor. He threw her into jail, and he also had bitter rows with his three sons Richard, John and Geoffrey. 99 (**C**)

D Exchequer

The Treasurer calculates taxes on a chequer board

The King

Chancery (The King's Chapel)

The Chancellor keeps the royal seal and gets the King's records written by the scribes

The King's Council A few powerful men who advise the King

Parliament (see page 34) Parliament is made up of the King's Council, barons, bishops, lords and burgesses

Sheriffs collect the taxes

Marshalls take orders for the army

Messengers carry orders from the King

Henry II, 1154-89

What kind of obituary might you write? You can choose to produce an account of Henry from the viewpoint of his bitter enemy, the King of France, or a loyal backer at court. In your obituary you can put drawings, maps and cartoons.

a Studying the sources (AT2, AT3)
1 A king could travel 10 miles a day. There were no roads as we know them, only tracks from one village or town to the next. Sea travel around Europe was in small sailing boats the size of an average classroom. What problems do you think Henry II faced in ruling his kingdom?
2 What ideas do you think the artist who drew **B** wants you to have about Henry? Is there any reason why the artist might have made Henry seem better or worse than he was?
3 Note down eight key words or ideas which **C** gives you about Henry. Is there any clue which suggests that we can trust what Gerald tells us about Henry?

4 Use **D** to explain how Henry might
• raise money to fight the King of France
• try a baron who has tried to kill him but who had been captured
• send out orders for his barons to bring their knights and footsoldiers to fight for him.

b Research (AT3). Find out what you can about Eleanor, Henry's wife. Read pages 24-25 to learn about Henry's awful quarrel with Thomas Becket.

c The Obituary (AT1). Use the information from your sources to write Henry's obituary. It should include:
• A headline
• Dates of his rule
• What he was like: looks, behaviour, personality
• Henry as a warrior
• How he ruled
• How he treated Queen Eleanor and his children
• His quarrel with Becket.

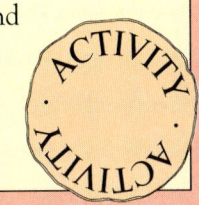

Crusader!

On 27 November 1095 the Pope, Urban II, preached a sermon which changed the history of the world. Fulcher of Chartres, a priest who was present, wrote down what the Pope said. Source **A** contains key extracts from the Pope's sermon:

> *Beloved brothers. I speak as a messenger to reveal to you God's will. We cannot refuse at once to give the help we have promised to our brothers in the East. They now need it desperately. The Turks and Arabs have attacked them and advanced into Romania... They have beaten the Christians seven times in battle, have killed and captured a large number of them, have wrecked their churches and laid waste to their land. If we do not go to help, the true servants of God in the East will not be able to survive.*
>
> *I therefore urge and beg you who are the voices of Christ, both rich and poor, to drive the foul vermin from the lands where your Christian brothers live and to bring speedy help to the worshippers of Christ... Promise your support without delay. Let the warriors get ready and find what they need to pay for the journey. When the spring comes let them leave in good spirit under the banner of the Lord.* **(A)**

(Fulcher of Chartres)

A crusader would travel across Europe and the Christian Byzantine Empire to the Holy Land. This is the area of the world we now call the Middle East. Jerusalem, the city where Jesus Christ was crucified, lies at the heart of the Holy Land. The Pope and most Christians felt that the Holy Land should be ruled by Christians. But the Holy Land was ruled by Arabs, whose religion was Islam. The Arab empire stretched along the Mediterranean and into southern Spain **(B)**. The Arabs had already tried to conquer

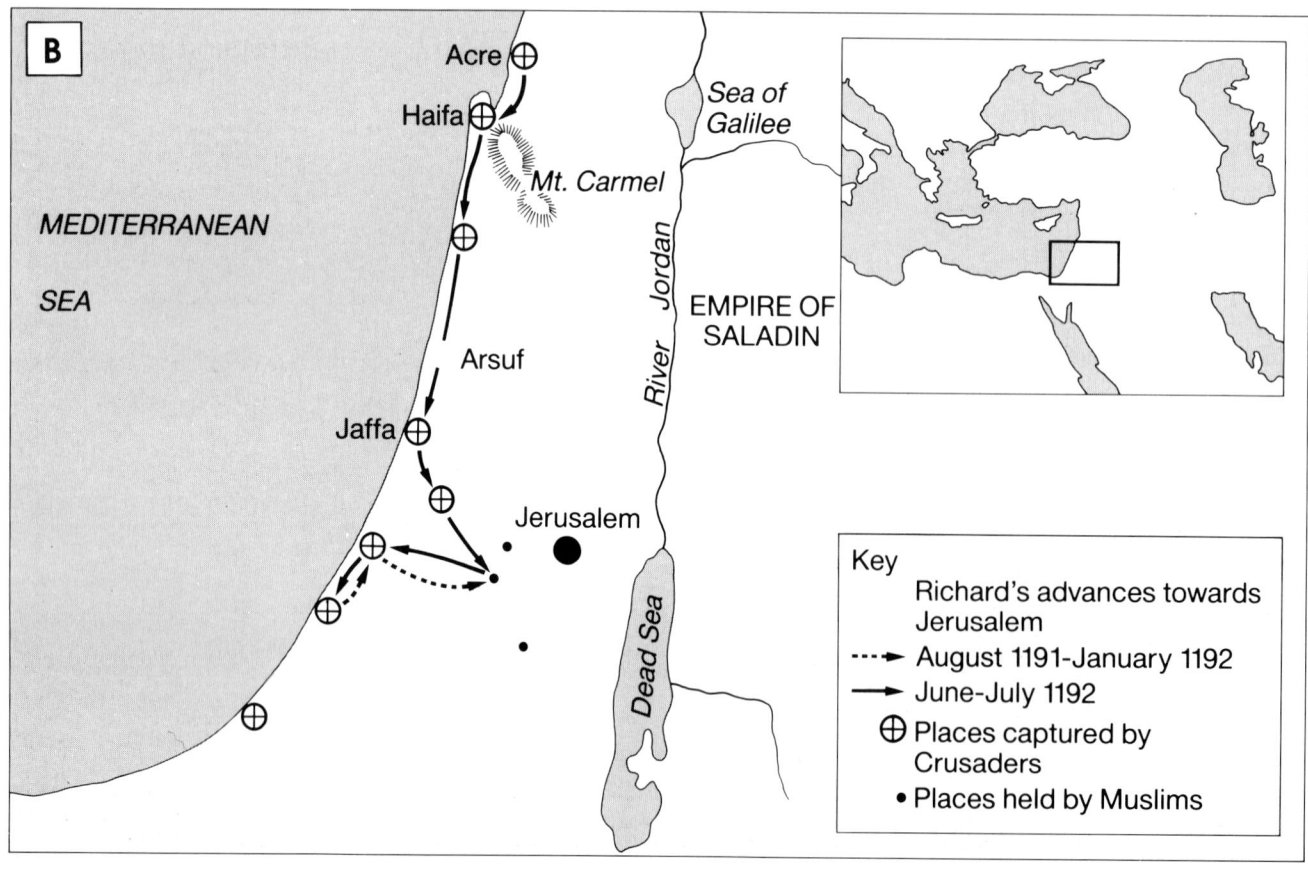

northern Spain, a Christian area. Many Christians already thought of the Arabs as enemies because they were Muslims.

In 1095 thousands flocked to answer the Pope's call (**A**). In 1099 the crusaders drove the Muslims out of Jerusalem with great slaughter. The crusaders split the Holy Land up into four kingdoms. For 70 years the crusaders fought off Arab attempts to drive them from their crusading kingdoms. The crusaders built strong castles, and seemed safe from attack. In the 1180s the Arabs found a new, strong leader, Saladin, who wiped out the crusaders' main army at the Battle of Hattin in 1187. Soon the crusaders had almost been pushed into the sea. A call for a new crusade went out from the Pope, and the Kings of Europe answered his plea. Richard the Lionheart led an English army, but he and his fellow kings failed to drive Arabs from Jerusalem. **C** shows him fighting Saladin. Other crusades followed, including the children's crusade of 1212, which involved peasants and children from the Rhineland and Southern France.

Going on a Crusade

Think of what you have to do when you go on holiday. What would it be like to go on a crusade in an age when you would have to travel on foot or horseback and by sailing boat, and when there were no modern roads, radio, telephone or tv? If you work as a group, you can split up tasks **b-e** between you.

a Read the message from the Pope (AT3). Is the sermon a genuine one? You decide to go on a crusade after hearing the Pope's sermon. List your reasons for going. What thoughts and feelings does the Pope have about the Turks and Arabs? Why might he think in this way?

b Planning the journey (AT1). Decide what things you will take with you, food, clothes, money, armour and weapons, **C**. What does **C** suggest about how the Arabs fought? How could you pay to support yourself while away from home?

c Design your own crusader banner or shield (AT1).

d The trip to Dover (AT1, AT3). You will sail from Dover. You go with a band of crusaders from your area. You can travel ten miles a day. Study pages 4-5, and use an atlas to work out your route. What will you see, where will you stay each night and what problems might you face on the journey?

e Disaster! (AT1). How you would behave if faced with these problems which you have heard about from earlier crusades?
- Your leader drowns while crossing a river.
- You are marching through the desert and Arab archers on horseback surround you.
- Two members of your band fall sick - remember there are no doctors and no modern hospitals.
- You run out of money and food in Asia Minor - there are no banks.

King John, 1199-1216

Bring in the prisoner! Here, in the court of History we are about to try King John. For hundreds of years King John has been accused of many crimes. Today historians think that he ruled England as well as most other medieval kings, and was no more cruel than they were. Read the evidence and make up your own mind.

CHARGE 1. John had brought shame on England through the loss of his lands in France, **A**.

The King of France drove John out of his lands in Northern France, including Normandy. This was a bitter blow. John fought hard, but was beaten by a better fighter. John's barons also betrayed him.

CHARGE 2. John was a wicked killer.

In 1202 John captured and threw into jail his nephew Arthur, ruler of Brittany. Arthur had plotted with the ruler of France to defeat John. A monk tells a story of Arthur's death (**B**). The monk lived in a Welsh Abbey owned by the soldier who captured and guarded Arthur.

❝ *At length in the castle of Rouen after dinner on the Thursday before Easter when he [John] was drunk and taken over by the Devil, he slew him [Arthur] with his own hand, and tying a heavy stone to the body cast it into the Seine. A fisherman found it in his net, and being dragged to the bank and recognised, the body was taken for secret burial.* ❞ (**B**)

(c 1205 The Chronicle of Margam)

CHARGE 3. John was an evil man because of the way he treated priests and nuns.

John had a dreadful quarrel with the Pope, for John claimed that he himself should run the Church in England. This included the right to say who should be bishops and hold other church posts. The Pope refused to accept John's claims, and then excommunicated him. This meant that John was no longer officially a Christian. He could not pray in church, be buried in a Christian grave or expect to go to heaven when he died. In return John grabbed Church lands and wealth and placed his own men in key Church posts. Long after John's death Roger of Wendover, a monk, tells us how John treated priests. I chose this extract because it is one of the best in making a precise charge against King John:

> *The King's men dragged priests of all kinds from their horses and robbed and beat them... The servants of a certain sheriff on the Welsh border brought to the King a robber they had caught. He had robbed and murdered a priest on the road. They asked the King what they should do with him. At once John replied, 'He has slain an enemy of mine, release him.'* (C)

D is from the Chronicle of Matthew Paris, and shows John's men torturing priests.

CHARGE 4. John lost the crown jewels in the Wash, a huge bay on the East coast of England.

John was crossing the Wash, with the baggage train carrying the Crown jewels following him. He had already reached dry land when he learned that the tide had come in and swamped the baggage train. Roger of Wendover tells us:

> *No one escaped to tell the King of the disaster.* (E)

John fought a long and bitter war against his barons. John lost the war, and in 1215 the barons forced him to accept the terms of Magna Carta, see pages 32-33. John kept on fighting his barons, but he died a year later after a meal of rough cider and unripe peaches.

The Trial of King John

We can try King John in the court of History. Decide who is to be the King, who will accuse him, and who will defend him.

Looking at the evidence (AT2, AT3).
In trying King John we have to look at the evidence. We can do this from two sides, the **prosecution** and the **defence**. You can split the charges up among you, dealing with one each.

For each of the **CHARGES** the prosecution must decide what might be said to show that John was guilty. The defence must decide what might be said to prove that he was innocent.

CHARGE 1.
Why was John to blame for the loss of the lands?
Was he a poor general?
Was the French King lucky?
Was the French King a good general?

CHARGE 2
Was Arthur in the wrong to plot against John?
Can we trust the Welsh chronicler? The extract from the monk's chronicle gives us a lot of detail.
Does this suggest anything to you?
Does the detail in the story strike us as being true?

Where is the body?

CHARGE 3
Is Roger of Wendover likely to be biased?
Is the story of the Welsh border true or not?
What facts back it up?
Was John to blame for how his men acted?

CHARGE 4
Had John been careless in crossing the Wash?
Who else might have been to blame?
What else might have happened?
Was it anyone's fault?

Having heard the evidence, say what kind of King you think John was.

Magna Carta

A pupil's charter of rights! How would you like to draw up an agreement between you and your parents and teachers which would give you as much freedom as you want? In 1215 the bishops and barons of England forced King John to accept such a charter. They hated King John because of the way that he had treated them (see page 30). The nobles' sole aim was to control the King. John had just lost a war against the French, so the bishops and barons seized their chance to make him agree to their terms. The King was forced to put his seal on Magna Carta, a treaty between him and his bitter enemies, in a meadow at Runnymede, **A**. Magna Carta is a long document written in Latin. It has 63 parts or clauses. Here are the main things that Magna Carta says:

1 The English church shall be free both to choose its own archbishops, abbots, bishops and priests and to run its own law courts.
2 As long as a guardian looks after a child, he shall use the money from the child's land to keep up the houses, park, fish ponds, other ponds, mills and the rest of the property.
3 The King shall not make an heir marry someone from a lower class.
4 The City of London shall have its old rights and freedoms, as will every other city, town and port.
5 The King shall get the backing of his archbishops, bishops, abbots, earls and great barons when he wants to raise money to fight a war.
6 The King's men will not try cases which only the Royal Judges should try.

A

7 The King will remove all fish weirs from all rivers. There will be the same weights and measures for wine, beer and corn throughout the land, and one width for dyed cloth.

8 No man shall be tried only upon the strength of what he has confessed. There must be witnesses who can be trusted.

9 No free man shall be jailed, stripped of what he owns or have force used against him (**B**) except by the law of the land.

10 The King will not accept bribes in court cases, nor delay them, nor deny anyone the right to be tried in court.

Today you are taught about Magna Carta because it has been used ever since to protect the rights of English people and to make sure that everyone gets a fair trial in court.

Magna Carta - Charter of Freedom!

You can draw up your own charter, both for today and for medieval times.

a Your grievances! (AT2)
1 By yourself, in pairs, groups and as a class work out a list of complaints against both your school and your parents.
2 Then draw up a list of rules to get rid of these grievances. This is your charter.
3 Make out your charter as if it was a medieval one, with a title at the top and a space for the signatures of witnesses at the bottom.

b Using the sources (AT3). Read through the list of points 1- 10 from Magna Carta.
1 Think hard about the *reasons* for each point in the charter. Say what each point suggests about how King John behaved towards his subjects. Discuss how the king and his men might have treated people in the area where you live.
2 Imagine you were alive in 1215. On a piece of paper, make out ONE grievance which you might have had against King John. Give examples of how you have been treated. You can do this as a picture like **B**.
3 Choose someone to be King John. Debate the grievances against him, and what he has to say about them.
4 Then draw up a charter between King John and one of these people who might have lived in your area:
• The baron
• A rich merchant
• A bishop
• A rich heir.

c Comparing Magna Carta with your own charter (AT2, AT1). Compare the points in your own charter with those of Magna Carta. How many are the same? Which of these rights laid down in Magna Carta do we enjoy today?
• Free speech
• Voting in elections
• Fair trial
• The right to be tried in court
• The right to own things, and not have them seized.

Parliament

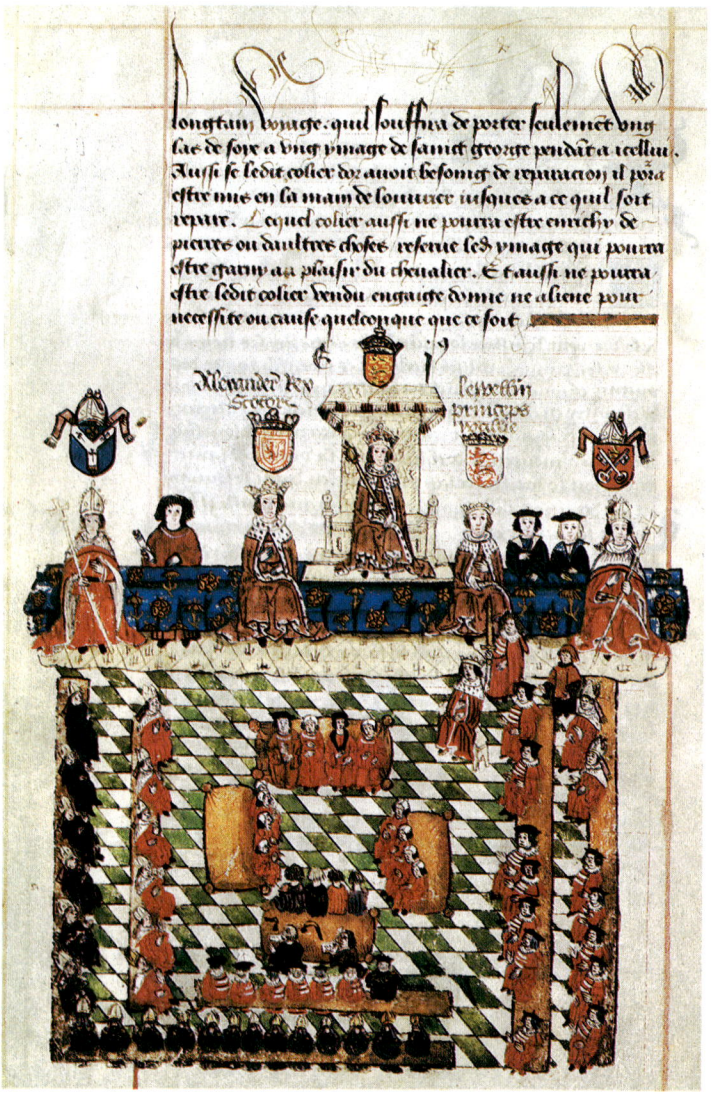

What did the medieval Parliament do? Sometimes Parliament would meet as a court to try cases - it was the most powerful court in England. The King could ask it to raise money through new taxes, money often needed to fight a war. He would also ask it to approve new laws. Source **A** is one of the earliest pictures of Parliament, and gives us some clues about how it worked.

Adam of Usk, a Welshman, wrote Source **B** about the meeting of Parliament in 1397-98. Adam tells us, "I, the writer of this chronicle, was present every day". The Parliament first met in London, and then moved to Shrewsbury. Its main work was to try rebels against the king and raise taxes. One case came across in a most vivid way. Try and work out what the source says. The English has not been changed:

❝ *21 September 1397. Richard, earl of Arundel, was put on his trial, clad in a robe of red with a hood of scarlet... Then rose up the earl of Derby and said to him, "Didst thou not say to me at Huntingdon where first we were gathered to revolt, that it would be better first of all to seize the king?" The earl replied: "Thou, earl of Derby, thou liest at they peril. Never had I thought concerning our lord the king, save what was to his welfare and honour". Then said the king to him, "Didst though not say to me,...*

FACTFILE

The word. Parliament gives us a clue about how Parliament started - *parley* means to talk, *ment* to act, Parliament was where the King could talk or parley with his powerful subjects and decide what to do.

Parliament's origins. Parliament grew out of the meetings of the King's Great Council (see page 13), those lords and bishops who helped him rule the country.

Simon De Montfort, 1258. King Henry III, a weak king, handed over power to a group of ruthless barons under Simon de Montfort who had seized power. To help Simon rule he called frequent meetings of the Great Council. Many barons hated Simon and refused to come.

De Montfort's Parliament -The first Parliament. Simon asked each county or shire to send two knights, and large towns to send two of its leaders or burgesses to Great Council meetings.

Edward I (1272-1307). Edward I was a strong king, see pages 46-50, 52-53. Edward carried on the idea of a Parliament of lords, knights and burgesses.

Two Houses of Parliament. In time Parliament split into two houses, the Lords and the Commons, and gained the powers it has today.

Where Parliament met. Parliament met where the King held his court, often in London.

History and Customs. Parliament has been meeting ever since, and still keeps many of its old customs. Find out about as many of these as you can.

Parliament Poster Contest

THE CONTEST A local museum is showing an exhibition on the History of Parliament. It is holding a contest for children to design a poster for schools about how Parliament was founded and what it did. You can enter the competition. To help design your poster use:
- the Factfile I worked out from a university historian's book on The Middle Ages
- sources **A** and **B**, and
- what else you can find out about Parliament's early days.

in the bath behind the White Hall, that Sir Simon Burley, my knight, was, for many reasons, worthy of death? And I answered thee that I knew no cause of death in him. And then thou and thy fellows did traitorously slay him." [The earl was found guilty and led to Tower Hill, where he was beheaded.]

[Then the Parliament moved to Shrewsbury] *28 January 1398. Then and there, too, the king wrung from the clergy a tenth and a half [a tax], and from the people a fifteenth and a half [a tax], and on every sack of wool five marks, and on every tun of wine five shillings, and on every pound's worth of merchandise two shillings, for the term of his life, amid the secret curses of his people.* 99 (B)

(The Chronicle of Adam of Usk, 1398)

a Poster design (AT1). You can by yourself, in pairs or groups prepare a poster. Your poster should announce the meeting of Parliament. On your poster show:

Who had called it	The King
Why he had called it	**a To raise money** to fight the French, see Source **B** for ideas.
	b To make a law to give control over the wool trade to major ports and towns.
	c To try one of his barons for treason against him. The baron has being fighting for the French King, and holds land from both him and the English King. Source **B** gives clues as to how the trial might have gone.
Who would be there?	The King, Lords and Bishops, Knights and Burgesses.
Where would it be held?	At the King's Court, in London

b Class Discussion (AT2, AT3).
1 Use your poster to introduce a class debate over the issues with which Parliament is dealing.
2 Split the form into different groups, The King and his ministers and the bishops, lords, knights and burgesses.
3 Each group works out its views on issues a-c at the time of the Peasants' Revolt, see page 36.
4 The King and his ministers put forward what they want, the other groups can argue against them.

The Peasants' Revolt

> *Robin Hood, Robin Hood, Riding through the Glen,*
> *Robin Hood, Robin Hood, with his band of men,*
> *Feared by the Bad, Loved by the Good,*
> *Robin Hood, Robin Hood, Robin Hood.*
> (A)

A is what I can remember of a folk song about a medieval hero whom we still talk about. Songs like it were sung about an event in 1381 which we still remember, The Peasants' Revolt. Why did the Peasants' Revolt break out in 1381? What went on in it, and how did it end?

Hunger and poverty played a big part. The medieval peasant scratched a living from the soil, and if the crops failed there was nothing to stop him and his family from starving. After the Black Death in 1348/49, see page 92, when one third of the peasants died and many villages were wiped out, peasants were often forced to work even harder for their lords.

Being poor is bad enough, but in 1380 things got worse when the government tried to force the peasants to pay more taxes. The government sent out tax collectors, and in May peasants at Brentwood in Essex refused to pay. Thousands of villagers joined them and cut off the heads of tax collectors they had captured. The revolt spread to Kent, **B**. Soon it found a leader in a priest who had just come out of gaol, John Ball, who preached that all men were equal.

On June 12 the peasants marched on London. By this time the counties around the capital had also burst into revolt. Another leader of the peasants, Wat Tyler, had emerged. The peasants reached London and soon took over the streets. On June 14 they killed two of the King's chief ministers.

> *All of whom they beheaded in the place called "Tourhille", without the said Tower; and then carrying their heads through the City upon lances, they set them up on London Bridge, fixing them there on stakes.* (C)

(City of London Letter Book 1381)

Things came to a head on June 15 when the King, Richard II, met the peasants. Use a dictionary to work out what source **D** says. Where did they meet? What happened? **E** is a clue. It shows what went on in **D**.

> *[William Walworth, the mayor of London] in Smithfield in presence of our Lord the King and those standing by him...on the one side, and the whole of this infuriated rout [mob] on the other, most manfully, by himself, rushed upon the captain of the said multitude, "Walter Tylere" by name, and, as he was arguing with the King and the nobles, first wounded him in the neck with his sword and then hurled him from his horse, with a deadly wound in the breast.* (D)

(City of London Letter Book 1381)

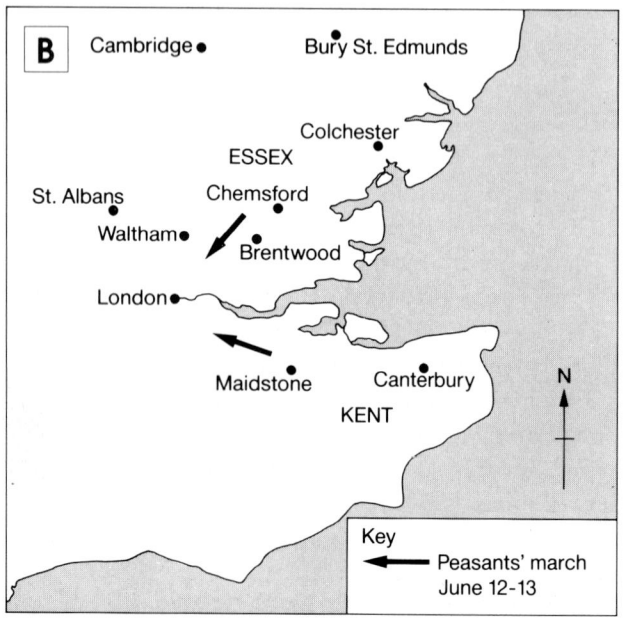

E

With the peasants' chief leader dead, Richard II got them to go home with promises that he would sort out and deal with their complaints. On July 2 he went back on his promises. Richard then used his army to round up the leaders of the Peasants' Revolt and peasants who still backed them. Soon across the South of England the gallows creaked with the weight of rotting bodies.

The Peasants' Revolt

You can use the facts and sources to write your own folk song or poem about the Peasants' Revolt.

a Timeline (AT1). Draw up a timeline of the main events of the revolt.

b Using the sources (AT3).
1 compare source D with picture E of the scene.
2 put sources C and D into your own words.

c Folk song (AT2). Decide what kind of folk song or poem you will write:
• from the point of view of a peasant or a peasant leader, OR
• from the point of view of the king or one of his nobles who crushed the revolt.

From this point of view, write two or three sentences saying what you think about: • Wat Tyler • Richard II • The mob in London.

Use these sentences in your song or poem. If you play a musical instrument you could also make up a tune for it.

Read out or sing your songs and poems as a class folk song event.

ACTIVITY · ACTIVITY

Joan of Arc

A gives clues about the 100 Years War, the life and death struggle between the English and French Kings which lasted from about 1350 to 1450. The war was fought over who should control French land. The contest swayed back and forth, **A**, until at last the French triumphed. In 1429 the French were losing, with the British on the attack. That year a great French leader arose, Joan of Arc. Who was Joan, a poor peasant girl?

The best account of Joan I could find was that of Jean Waverin, a French chronicler who lived at the time. Waverin tells us how Joan came to the French king's court saying that God had sent her to lead the French to victory against the English:

> *She was very bold in riding horses and leading them to drink... And she was thought of at court as being mad and mistaken, because she boasted that she could achieve so great a task which the great princes had thought impossible. However, after the maid had stayed a long time at the king's court... she was brought forward and helped, and she raised a banner, her standard on which she had painted the figure and likeness of Our Lord Jesus Christ.* **(B)**
>
> (Jean Waverin c 1435)

Joan, dressed in armour, won some skirmishes against English troops, and built up a strong force of French soldiers. Source C is a later French picture of Joan leading her men. The English army was besieging the major French city of Orléans. Joan led a French force against the English. The Tourelles, an English fort on an island, **D,** was the key to English plans to capture Orléans. The French attacked the earthwork leading to the island, but were forced back. A Frenchman, Aulon, fought alongside Joan. He wrote that as the French were about to retreat he decided to attack with Joan's standard bearer, a Basque:

FACTFILE

A THE 100 YEARS WAR

1 English land in France in 1327 →

2 1340 The Battle of Sluys: an English fleet destroys a French fleet

3 1347 Calais gained by the English after the smashing victory of Crécy

4 1360 Major gains of land for the English after they capture the French King at the Battle of Poitiers →

5 1360-1415 The French fight back, and the English lose all the lands they gained

6 1415 Agincourt. Henry V, King of England, crushes the French King's forces in a battle in which the English archers slaughter the heavily armoured French knights

7 1415-22 The area which Henry V gained →

8 1420s and 30s Under Joan of Arc the French drive the English back. In 1431 the English burn Joan of Arc as a witch. Joan had been captured and handed over to them

9 1431-53 The French continue to drive back the English, finally leaving the English king with the port of Calais

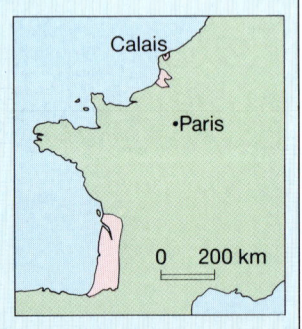

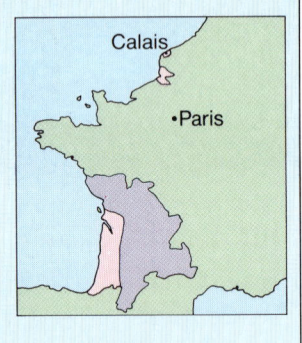

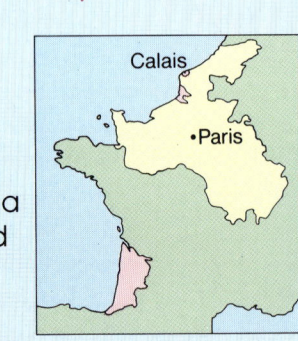

C

> *But when the Maid saw her standard in the hands of the Basque, she was afraid that she had lost it. For he was by now in the ditch. She then seized her standard by the pole so firmly that he could not hold it, crying, "Ha, my standard, my standard!" And she shook her standard so hard that I imagined others might suppose she was making a sign to them... Whereupon all the Maid's army rushed together and immediately charged.* **(E)**

Joan's troops stormed the Tourelles from one side, while French troops in the town managed to set fire to the drawbridge linking it to the shore. The English commander was caught up in the flames and tumbled into the river where he drowned. Soon the English were driven back from Orléans, one in a long line of French successes, see Factfile **A**.

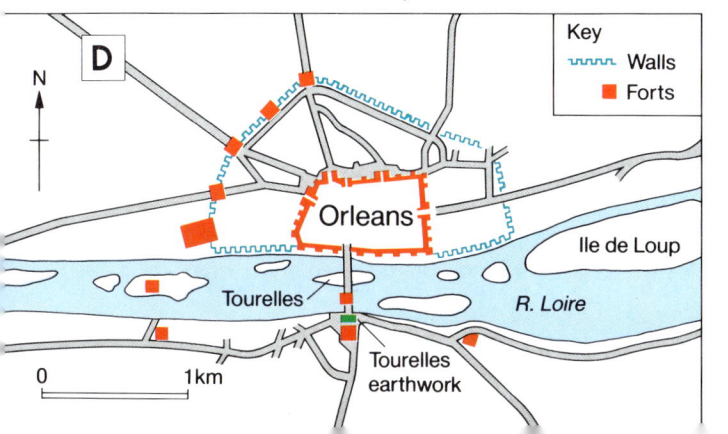

D (map of Orléans showing walls, forts, Tourelles, Tourelles earthwork, Île de Loup, R. Loire)

The 100 Years War

You can use the sources to design your own banner for Joan, and a poster or wall display about her role in beating the English. Draw your poster from EITHER the English OR the French point of view.

a The banner (AT3). Read **B**. Decide upon the shape, what picture or sign you will draw, and any motto that you would like to put on it.

b The poster or wall display (AT1, AT3). The poster will tell the story of Joan of Arc, and the part she played in beating the English. You can split the poster/wall display jobs up among you. Mark on your poster:

1 The area of France in English hands in 1429 (**A**). On the map you can mark key events of the war.
2 The problems which the French faced after the defeat of Agincourt (**A**).
3 A picture or cartoon of Joan coming to the French court to convince the king that God had sent her to save his kingdom.
4 A picture or account of Joan leading French troops against the English at Orléans (Sources **C**, **D** and **E**).
5 The English burning Joan as a witch.

c Wall display (AT2). Put up your posters as a wall display. How do they differ in their views of Joan? In what ways are they similar?

ACTIVITY

The Wars of the Roses

We still talk about The Wars of the Roses. Before you read on, say how you think they got their name, and what the wars were about. From the mid-15th century two great noble families fought over which of them should rule England. These two families, York and Lancaster, later took as their badges a white or a red rose. The War Graph, **A,** helps you see how the struggle went. There were long periods of peace, after which fierce fighting broke out for a few weeks. At the end of the fighting England had a new ruler.

Both great families, York and Lancaster, relied on other nobles who had their own armies. The struggle for power lasted until around 1500, when a new ruling family, the Tudors, had firm control over England - see page 45.

Do you have a family photo album, or a scrapbook of things that have happened in the past? The Pastons were a land-owning family who lived at the time of the Wars of the Roses. A large number of their family papers survive. They show how the Wars of the Roses might have affected the lives of people who lived on their lands. You can use these sources to make up an entry for a Paston family scrapbook.

In 1448-9 Lord Moleyns, another land owner with his own private army, claimed that he, and not the Pastons, was the owner of their manor house, lands and villages at Gresham in Norfolk. Moleyns attacked the Pastons in 1448. Try and puzzle out the meaning of Margaret Paston's letter asking for help. It has not been changed, it is very much an original source:

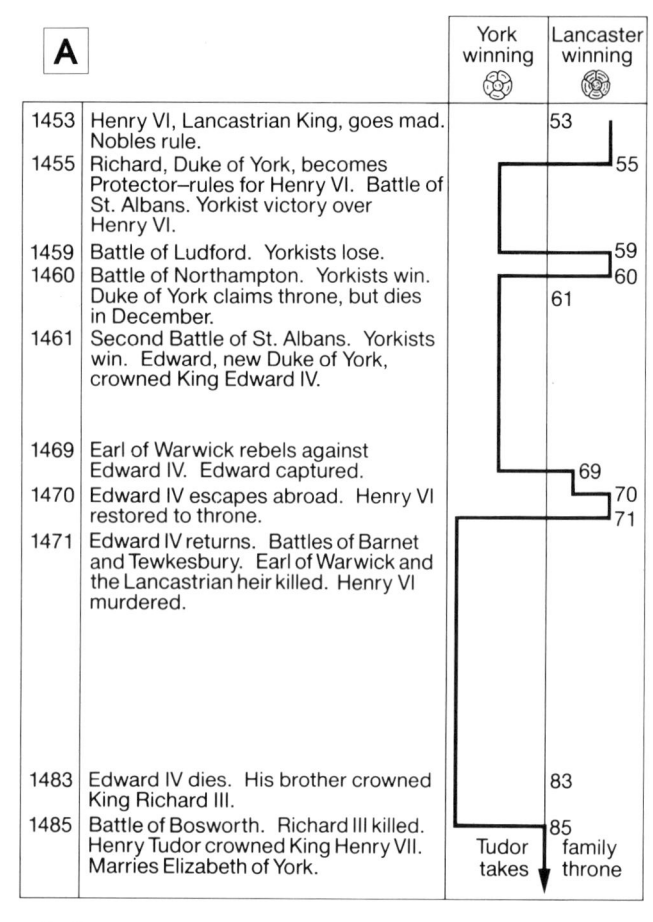

A

Year	Event	York winning	Lancaster winning
1453	Henry VI, Lancastrian King, goes mad. Nobles rule.		53
1455	Richard, Duke of York, becomes Protector–rules for Henry VI. Battle of St. Albans. Yorkist victory over Henry VI.	55	
1459	Battle of Ludford. Yorkists lose.		59
1460	Battle of Northampton. Yorkists win. Duke of York claims throne, but dies in December.	60 61	
1461	Second Battle of St. Albans. Yorkists win. Edward, new Duke of York, crowned King Edward IV.		
1469	Earl of Warwick rebels against Edward IV. Edward captured.	69	
1470	Edward IV escapes abroad. Henry VI restored to throne.		70 71
1471	Edward IV returns. Battles of Barnet and Tewkesbury. Earl of Warwick and the Lancastrian heir killed. Henry VI murdered.		
1483	Edward IV dies. His brother crowned King Richard III.	83	
1485	Battle of Bosworth. Richard III killed. Henry Tudor crowned King Henry VII. Marries Elizabeth of York.	85 Tudor takes	family throne

> *Right worshipful husband, I recommend me to you, and pray you to get some crossbows and wyundases* [windlasses to wind back the bow-string] *and quarrels* [heavy arrows for crossbows]; *for your houses here are so low that no man may shoot out there with any long bow, though we had never so much need...* [the letter asks for poleaxes and talks about the house's defences and then goes on] *I pray that you will vouchsafe to have bought for me 1lb of almonds and 1lb of sugar, and that you will have some frieze bought with which to make your children's gowns. And I pray that you would buy a yard of broad cloth of black for a hood for me.* **(B)**

(Margaret Paston to John Paston)

On the 28 January 1449, Lord Moleyns captured another of the Paston family's houses. The Pastons asked Parliament for help:

A Family Scrapbook

You can plan out and make an entry for a Wars of the Roses scrapbook. Imagine **you** are living with the Pastons as a member of the family. First work through **a**, then put in one or more of the other scenes or stories **b**, **c** or **d**. You can split the tasks up among you to produce a family scrapbook.

a Handling the sources (AT3).
1 Look carefully at **D**, and describe all the things going on in the picture. On what do you think the picture is based?
2 Work out what **B** means. Pick out words you do not understand and look them up in a dictionary. Puzzle out what the sentences mean, then write out the letter for help in modern English. Do the same for source **C**, and put both in your scrapbook.

b Attack on your house (AT1). Imagine you were living during the Wars of the Roses, and that your house was about to be attacked. Draw a plan of how you would fortify it against attacks like the one in **C**.
c The enemy attack (AT1). Based upon C, make an entry in your scrapbook of what happened when the enemy force attacked and stormed your house, and threw you into the street, or draw a picture like **D** of what went on.
d Your wrecked home (AT1). Use sources **C** and **D** to make a list of what had happened to your house when you returned home after the enemy had left.
e Design (AT1). Design a night gown for a five year old child and a medieval hood made out of black cloth, to be worn at night while fleeing from an enemy. Put the design in your scrap-book.

ACTIVITY · ACTIVITY

> *The said lord sent to the said mansion a riotous people, to the number of 1,000 persons, arrayed [dressed] in manner of war, with cuirasses, brigandines, jacks, salets, swords, bows, arrows, large shields, guns, pans with fire and faggots burning therein, long crooks to pull down houses, ladders, picks, with which they mined down the walls, and long trees with which they broke up gates and doors, and came into the said mansion, the wife of your beseecher at the time being therein, and 12 persons with her; the which persons they drove out of the said mansion, and mined down the wall of the chamber wherein the wife of your said beseecher was, and bore her out at the gates, and cut assunder the posts of the houses and let them fall.* **(C)**

(John Paston's petition to Parliament, 1450)

The house was wrecked and looted, **D** suggests how, and the Pastons were driven from their land. Local feuds between families like the Pastons and Moleyns often linked in to the struggles between the families of York and Lancaster. The Pastons backed the Lancastrians. Can you think how they tried to win back their lands from enemies who backed the Yorkists?

Murder!

No bodies, only ugly rumours. The two young boys may not even have been killed! If they were murdered, who did it, when, why, how? How might a journalist, working for a children's TV programme, go about finding out what happened to the children? First look at the Factfile and then sources **A-E**.

We can look at two key sources from the time. In the Great Chronicle of London, a Londoner wrote down what he heard from others (**A**). The report of Thomas More (**B**), written some 30 years later, needs treating with great care. Thomas lived as a lad with one of Richard III's most bitter enemies and worked at the courts of Kings Henry VII and Henry VIII. Henry VII defeated Richard at the Battle of Bosworth and replaced Richard as king.

> *And during this mayor's year [October 1482 - October 1483] the children of King Edward were seen shooting and playing in the garden of the Tower at sundry times. All the winter season of the next mayor's time [1483-84] the land was in good quiet, but after Easter [1484] there was much whispering among the people that the king had put the children of King Edward to death.... some said that they were murdered between two feather beds, some said that they were drowned in malmsey [a wine], and some said that they were pierced with a venomous potion.... Sir James Tyrell was reported to be the doer, but others put that weight upon an old servant of King Richard's.* **(A)**

(Robert Fabian 1484, *The Great Chronicle of London*)

> *Tyrell decided that the Princes should be murdered in their beds the next night, and chose Miles Forest and John Dighton to do the job. Forest was one of the Princes' guards and had already murdered others; Dighton was a big, broad, strong fellow. About midnight they entered the chamber where the children lay asleep in their beds. They pressed the feather beds and pillows hard on the children's faces until they stopped breathing, and fetched Sir James Tyrell to see them... This story is well known to be true, because when Sir James Tyrell was imprisoned in the Tower in 1502 for treason against King Henry VII, both he and Dighton were questioned. They confessed that they had done the murder in the way I have described.* **(B)**

(Sir Thomas More 1513 *History of Richard III*)

FACTFILE

The children. The two children, Edward and Richard, were the young sons of Edward IV (1461-83). The oldest child, Prince Edward, would have become King when he grew up.

Their possible enemies. Three people would have gained from their deaths: Richard III, the Duke of Buckingham and Henry Tudor.

Richard III was the princes' uncle, and would be an obvious winner from their deaths - he would be King!

The Duke of Buckingham, who also wanted to be King, was in London when they disappeared and could have killed them. In 1484 he headed a rising against Richard III, was defeated and beheaded.

Henry Tudor. If the princes had still been alive in 1485, they would have had a better claim to the throne than Henry.

Richard's defenders. They claim that there is no evidence which actually proves Richard killed the Princes in the Tower. They believe that none of the accounts would stand up today in a court of law as proof that Richard had the children murdered.

The bones. Bones of two young children were found buried at the bottom of the staircase in the tower (**E**). Doctors tell us the bones were from the bodies of 9-14 year old children and that there is no way of knowing when they were buried. The remains might have been those of two other children, but they are quite likely to be the bones of the princes.

C is the princes' family tree. D is what a Victorian artist thinks happened to them. On what do you think he based the picture?

A TV Reporter Investigates the Princes' Disappearance

What programme might you produce about the children's disappearance? You can work by yourself, with a friend, or in a group on the following ideas.

a The Evidence (AT3).
1 In the office you have a file of cuttings about the deaths of the Princes. The cuttings contain the Factfile and sources **A-E**. To help you, visit the library or consult any books you can find about the Princes' disappearance.
2 Your TV programme can take one of three viewpoints:
• that Richard III killed the princes, or
• that someone else carried out the crime, or
• that we can't tell what happened to them.
In each case you have to study the evidence to work out how it can be **used to support your story**.

b Your story (AT1, AT2).
Your story may include:
• The Programme Title and headlines.
• A timeline, a facts table with brief, one line accounts of the characters and the key events, and a family tree. You could include the consequences of the killings and who gained most from the deaths.
• Plans and drawings, including a cartoon account of what happened.
• Imaginary interviews with those involved, Richard III, Henry VII, Fletcher and Dighton, Tyrell, Buckingham.
• A re-creation of how the crime was carried out - remember that the killers would have needed permission to get into the tower to commit the crime. Brainstorm key words about the crime and use them in your TV drama. Here is a short list to start you off:
steps; clank; drip; rats; squeak; beds; pillows; fight; screams; struggle; bodies; spades; flagstones.
• A look at the evidence to see how much trust can be placed on it.

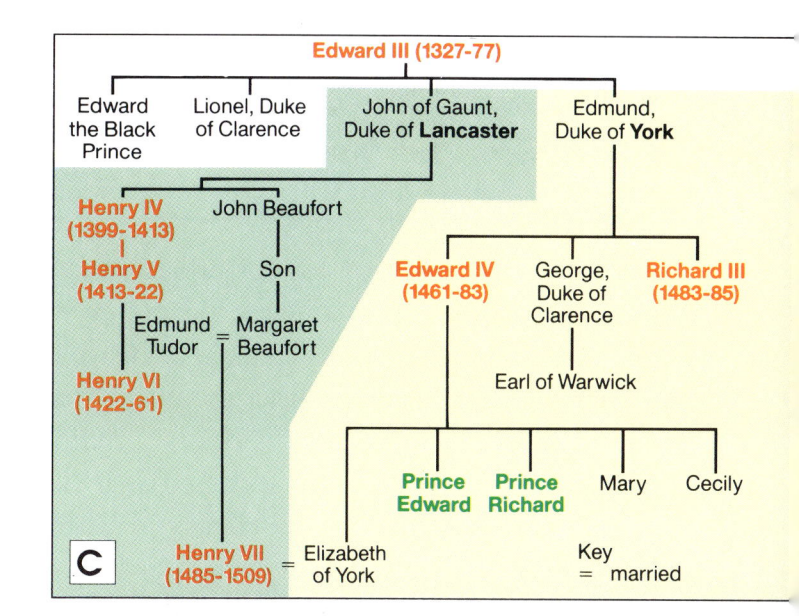

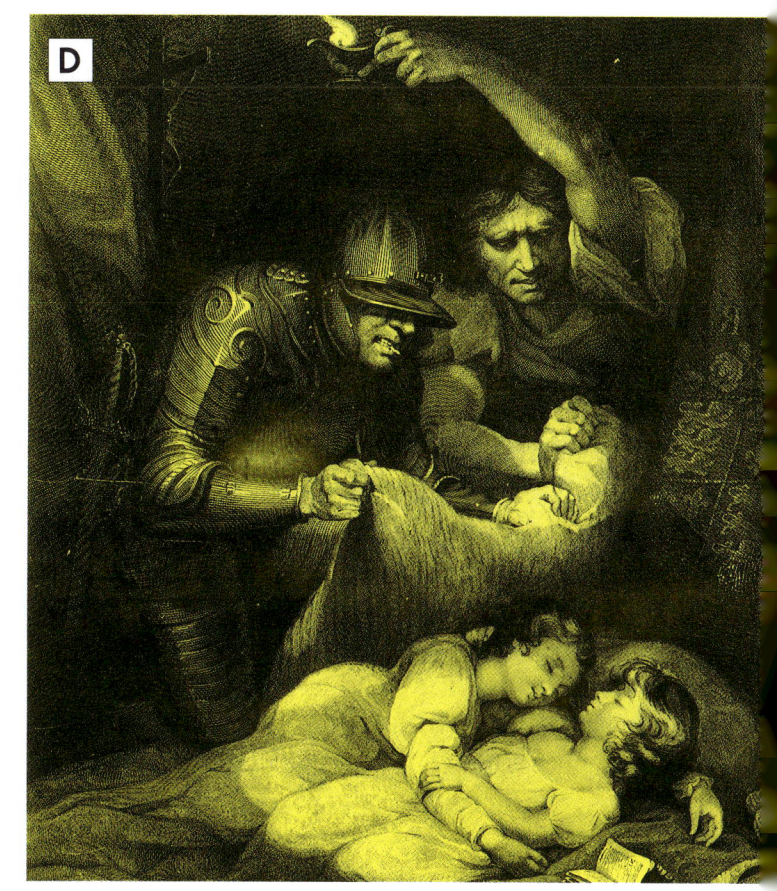

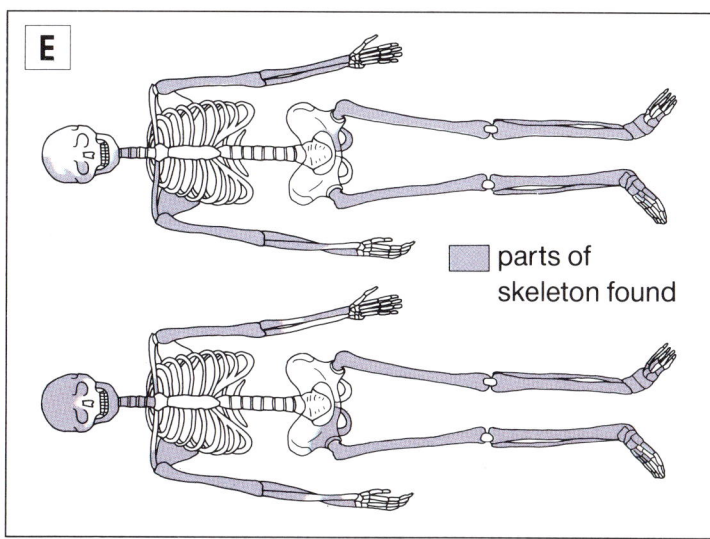

ACTIVITY

C

Edward III (1327-77)
— Edward the Black Prince
— Lionel, Duke of Clarence
— John of Gaunt, Duke of **Lancaster**
— Edmund, Duke of **York**

Henry IV (1399-1413) — John Beaufort
Henry V (1413-22) — Son
Edmund Tudor = Margaret Beaufort
Henry VI (1422-61)

Edward IV (1461-83) — George, Duke of Clarence — Richard III (1483-85)
Earl of Warwick

Prince Edward   Prince Richard   Mary   Cecily

Henry VII (1485-1509) = Elizabeth of York

Key
= married

D

E

parts of skeleton found

The Battle of Bosworth

On radio you can hear lots of programmes about the past. Look in a newspaper to see if there are any on tonight. To make a history programme the producer asks an author to write a script. You can help work out a radio programme on Henry Tudor and the Battle of Bosworth. At Bosworth Henry Tudor defeated the English King, Richard III. During the battle Richard was killed, and Henry Tudor became the new king, Henry VII. The Factfile gives you the background to the Battle. My account of the Battle is based on our best source, the writings of Polydore Vergil, who lived at the time but was not present at Bosworth.

The Battle of Bosworth. Richard had an awful nightmare the night before the battle which told him he would die next day. In the morning Richard drew up his army on Ambien Hill, **B**. Henry Tudor's army was at the bottom of the hill. The two armies moved towards each other and clashed in mid morning, when Richard ordered his men to charge after firing a volley of arrows. Richard and his knights made for Henry's standard, aiming to cut Henry down. They managed to topple Henry's standard and kill the standard bearer and Henry's strongest knight. Henry was on the brink of defeat.

At this point the army of the Stanleys charged Richard's men. Attacked on two sides, many of Richard's troops fled. King Richard was cut down in the fighting. **A** is a picture which was drawn some 50 years later. I picked it to give a feel of hand-to-hand fighting. Richard's battered crown was found lying on the battle field and placed on Henry's head. The Great Chronicle of London tells us what happened to Richard's body, which:

FACTFILE

Richard III as King. Like most successful medieval kings Richard was a callous killer. He slaughtered or jailed any great nobles who stood in his way. One he had even dragged out of a meeting of his ministers and beheaded on the spot! So, by 1485 he had made many strong enemies, itching for revenge.

Richard III v Henry Tudor. The biggest threat to Richard III was Henry Tudor who had fled to France. Henry was the Lancastrian heir to the throne, see page 42.

Lords and Barons. England was a country of great lords and barons, each of whom had his own army. Richard III had his own troops who lived on the lands he owned, but the bulk of his army was made up from the soldiers of his nobles, nobles such as the Duke of Norfolk, who played a huge part in the Battle of Bosworth.

Henry Tudor's support. Henry's family was from Wales. Henry thought that Wales was the best place to raise soldiers to fight Richard III before marching to attack him. So, Henry landed on 7 August 1485 at Milford Haven in South Wales, an area which his uncle Jasper ruled.

The march to Bosworth. From Milford Haven Henry set out to conquer England. On his way many local knights and lords flocked to his banner. Soon his small force had swollen into a strong army. The two forces drew near at Bosworth in Leicestershire.

Before the Battle. Three armies were present at the battle on the 22 August 1485: those of Henry Tudor and Richard III, and a third force, that of the Stanley family. Richard had twice as many men as Henry, whose army was a little bigger than that of the Stanleys. The Stanleys were a great noble family; who would they back in the battle? They hated Richard, who had some of their family with him as hostages.

> *was that afternoon brought into that town, Leicester. For his body was despoiled to the skin, and nothing was left about him so much as would cover his privy member, and he was trussed behind a pursuivant called Norroy as a hog or other vile beast. And so all bespattered with mire and filthy he was brought to a church in Leicester for all men to wonder upon, and was there finally irreverently buried.* (C)

(The Great Chronicle of London 1485)

England now had a new ruling family, the Tudors.

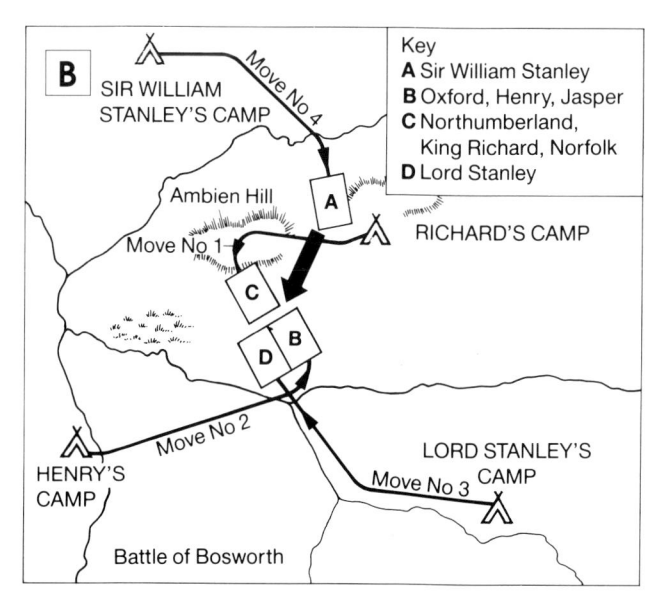

Key
A Sir William Stanley
B Oxford, Henry, Jasper
C Northumberland, King Richard, Norfolk
D Lord Stanley

Battle of Bosworth

Radio Programme on the Battle of Bosworth

In planning your radio programme you will need to write a script. You can use the text and any other sources in the way I suggest below, or you can work out your own plan. You can share out the work between you, with different people planning different scenes for the programme.

Radio Programme - outline. Narrator and interviews.

a Background to invasion - narrator (AT1). The thoughts and feelings of Henry. Interviews with people on the ship and Jasper Tudor. Thoughts about Richard III.

b Landing at Milford (AT1). Interview with Henry. Reasons for invasion. Claim to the throne.

c The night before Bosworth (AT1). Narrator talks about the two camps of Richard and Henry, how the leaders and their noblemen feel, and the views of the common soldiers.

d Interview with the Stanleys (AT1). Before the battle, ask them which side they intend to back (if they will tell you) and why. Their story of the contacts between them and Richard and Henry.

e The battle (AT3). Using **A** and **B**, produce an account of different battle scenes during the struggle - the start of the battle, the attack on Henry's standard, the Stanleys join in, death of Richard.

f After the battle (AT3). Interview the author of **C**, asking whether he actually saw the body, what other details he knew, the burial of Richard's corpse.

g Tape (AT1). Tape record your story of the Bosworth campaign and battle.

Edward I and Wales

Conquering Wales

Today advisers help politicians make decisions. They have to look at all the evidence, much of it historical, to make up their minds. How would you do as a political adviser to Edward I? You can work through each of the four problems on the next three pages, or split them up among you and then pool your ideas on what you would have advised Edward to do. Edward's actual decisions are given at the foot of p 48.

ACTIVITY

My eleven-year-old daughter Eleanor wrote an imaginary interview with Adam of Usk. Adam was a Welshman who kept a chronicle of what happened in Wales 100 years after the reign of Llywelyn, Wales' first great leader. Eleanor asked Adam questions about Wales and Llywelyn, and worked out his possible replies, using a history book to help her:

Eleanor Who ruled Wales 100 years before you wrote your chronicle?

Adam In each part of the land a local lord ruled, with his own band of fighting men. The Welsh soldiers wore little armour, fought with daggers, spears, swords and bows and arrows and were clever at ambushes. They moved quickly, mounted on their small, sturdy ponies. When attacked, they could retreat to strong forts, often on hill tops or hidden in the forest.

Eleanor Who was Llewelyn?

Adam In the 1260s the strongest of the Welsh lords, Llywelyn, Prince of Wales, fought local lords and the English to build up a strong kingdom (**A**). Llywelyn made peace with the English in 1267. This peace lasted for ten years, but by 1277 Llywelyn was on the war path.

Eleanor Why should he go to war with the English? His kingdom seems big enough.

Adam Llywelyn refused to pay homage (see page 22) to King Edward I of England (1272-1307). This made Edward furious. In turn Edward had seized the ship carrying Llywelyn's bride to Wales, which made Llywelyn hopping mad. Llywelyn also feared Edward would back his brother David's plot to kill him.

Eleanor I notice on the map (**A**) that around Llywelyn's lands were strung five great lordships of King Edward. What were these marcher lordships?

Adam The king gave his great lords huge areas, lordships, to rule in return for fighting for him when asked. These strong barons ruled their lordships with their own large, private armies of knights and footsoldiers. The barons' knights itched to get their hands on Welsh lands.

Problem 1. How to invade Wales (AT1)

Study map **A**. What sort of land is Wales? Would it be easy for a big army to fight there? Knowing how the Welsh fight, if you were one of the marcher lords or Queen Eleanor (Edward's wife) advising the King, would you suggest that he should:

1a Invade Wales from Chester along the coast with a single large army. Ships would keep the army supplied. OR
1b Get the Marcher lords to mount three attacks, one from Montgomery, the second into Brecon and the third into Cardigan OR
1c Carry out plan **a** then plan **b** OR
1d Carry out plan **b** then plan **a** OR
1e Carry out plan **a** and plan **b** together OR
1f Some other plan

Write out which of the plans you would recommend Edward to follow. Then in the form of a diary, letter or speech say how you think the campaign went.

ACTIVITY

ELEANOR Adam, how did things work out?

ADAM Bitter fighting raged throughout 1277, and Llywelyn, driven back but not beaten, made peace. Edward forced him to accept a cut-down kingdom around Snowdon. To keep a grip on Llywelyn Edward built four new castles at Flint, Rhuddlan, Aberystwyth and Builth Wells. Can you think why he chose these four sites?

ELEANOR What happened then?

ADAM Peace lasted for four years, with terrible quarrels between the British and Welsh on how much land the Welsh were to hand over to the English. In 1282 fighting broke out over land. The Welsh rushed to fight against Edward, with Llywelyn as their leader. The Welsh rising was a disaster. Edward invaded with a strong army from Rhuddlan (see map A). Two other English armies under marcher lords stormed into Wales from Carmarthen and Montgomery. Llywelyn rushed South to whip up support against the English, and attacked Builth castle. In a skirmish with some English troops an English soldier skewered Llywelyn on his spear (B), and so died The Prince of Wales.

ELEANOR Is that the end of the story?

ADAM Llywelyn's death knocked the stuffing out of the Welsh fighters. By 1284 all of Wales was in Edward I's hands, and at Rhuddlan the Welsh were forced to sign a peace treaty.

Edward pressed on with building his castles and making sure that the Welsh obeyed their English rulers (see problems 3 and 4, page 48). The Welsh have never forgotten Llewellyn, the last leader of their free nation.

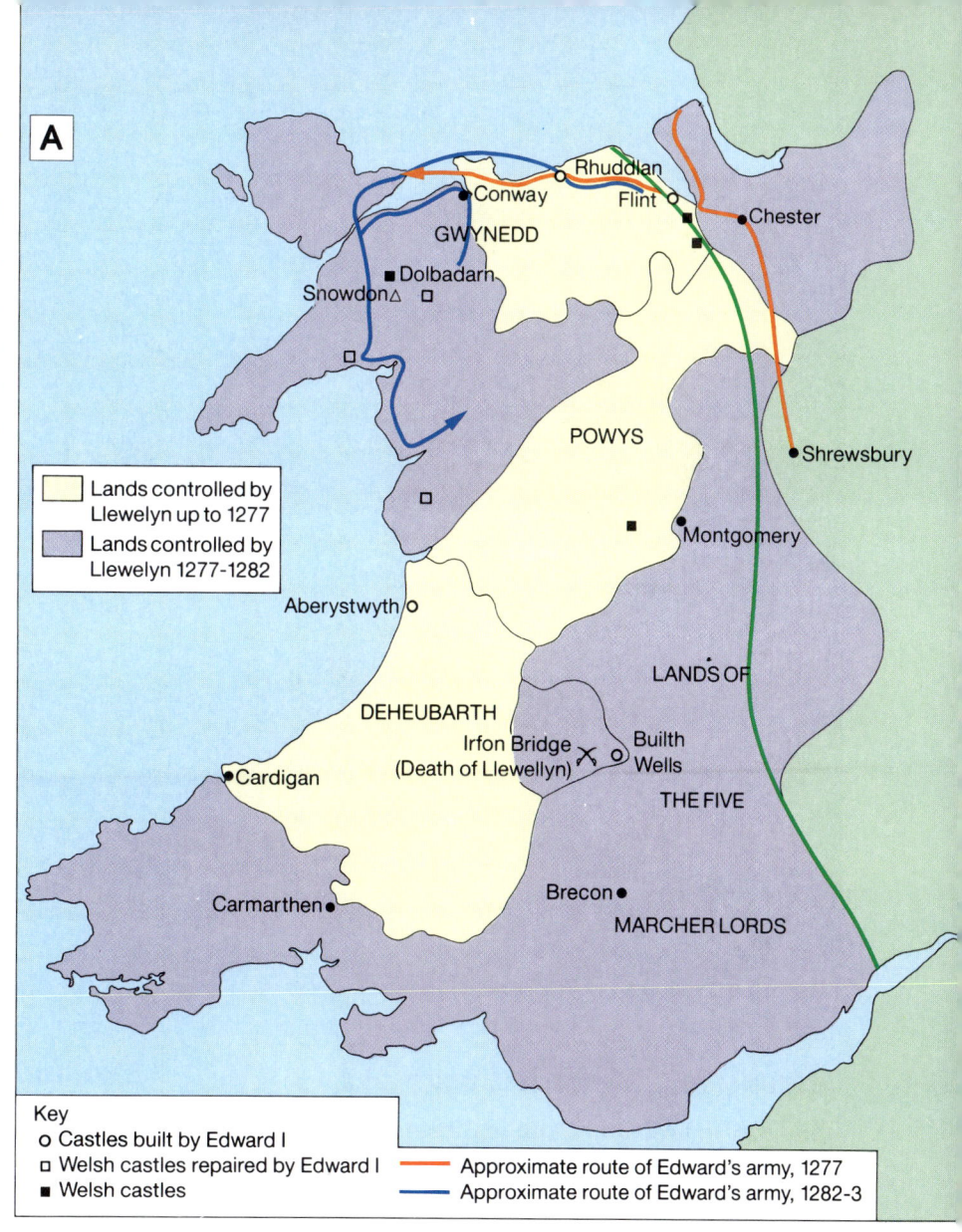

Problem 2. A Welsh Peace Treaty (AT1)

If you were advising Edward on the treaty of Rhuddlan, would you advise him to:

2a Split Wales up into huge lordships, keeping the principality of Snowdonia, Cardigan and Carmarthen for himself. There is always the danger of making his own lords too strong. OR

2b Divide Wales up into small lordships, giving some back to the Welsh and the rest to his own barons and knights. This would make control easy in times of peace, but the Welsh might rally under a new strong leader and drive the English out. OR

2c Follow some other plan.

Copy map **A** and mark on it how you would divide Wales up in 1284, and explain your plan. Draw up a peace treaty for the Welsh to sign.

Problem 3. Welsh Laws (AT1)

In order to keep the Welsh in order Edward needed to make sure that they obeyed the law. What laws would you suggest?

3a The old laws of Wales, with Welsh nobles making sure they were obeyed.
3b The laws of England, with English courts to enforce them.
3c New laws.

If you choose **3c** draw up a set of laws for Edward, to keep the Welsh under control.

ACTIVITY ACTIVITY

Problem 4. Siting Castles (AT1)

Where would you build **four** new, strong castles to add to those Edward had already built? Think about these points when siting your new castles:

4a They should be at the mouth of a river. Ships are small enough to sail up the river to dock at the castle. This means that the castle can hold out for a long time against any siege.
4b They should control a large area of low land. This would mean that under the castle's control would be local villages and areas where the Welsh grow grain and raise cattle.
4c The castles should be about 30 miles apart. Fifteen miles is the distance an armed force can travel on foot in one day.
4d One castle should be on Anglesey. Anglesey is the bread basket of Wales. Any Welsh army needs grain from Anglesey to feed its men when on campaign. Cut off the corn, and the Welsh can't fight.
4e They should be on the coast of Llywelyn's old principality of Snowdonia. His ex-stronghold is the most likely place for a Welsh rising in the future.

Draw up a plan for the siting of the castles, and mark where you would put them on an outline map of Wales.

ACTIVITY ACTIVITY

Edward's decisions

Problem 1. Edward followed plan 1d with great success.
Problem 2. Snowdon remained in Edward's hands, other areas were given to Edward's marcher barons. Wales was split up into counties, each centred on a major castle, and run in the same way as English counties.
Problem 3. Edward introduced the English law, and English judges and courts.
Problem 4. Edward had already built Builth, Rhuddlan, Flint and Aberystwyth - although Aberystwyth had been burned down in the war. He then built four new royal castles, Beaumaris, Carnarvon, Conway and Harlech, and backed them up with a network of small forts and castles in the hands of his nobles, such as those at Denbigh. Next to many of these castles the English founded towns.

Concentric Castle

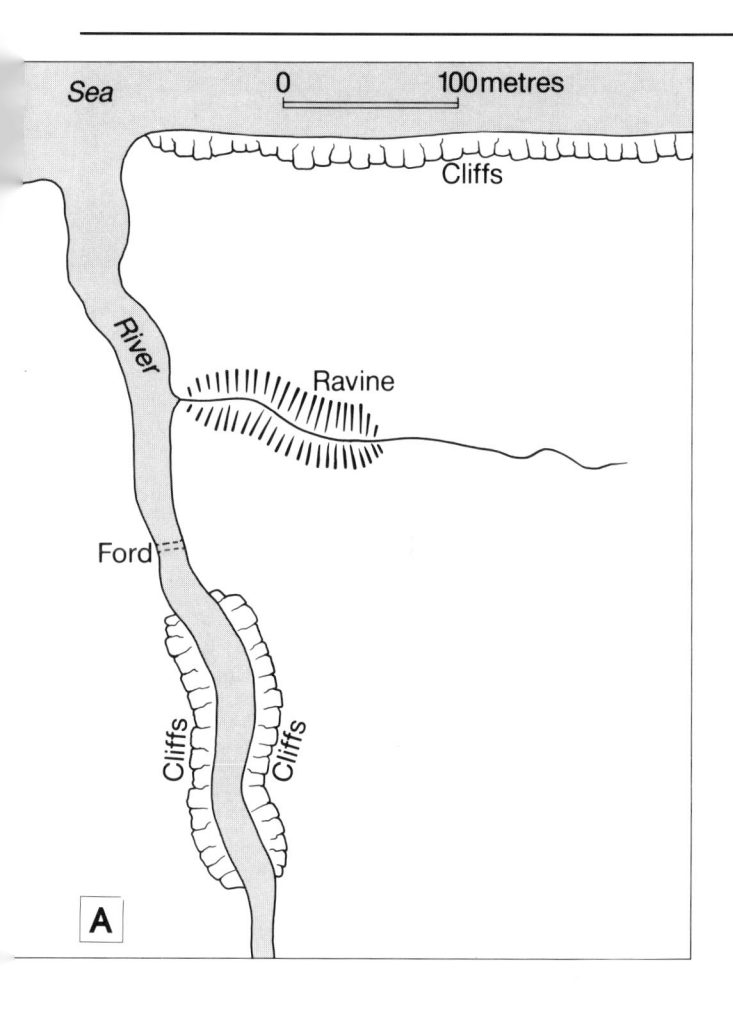

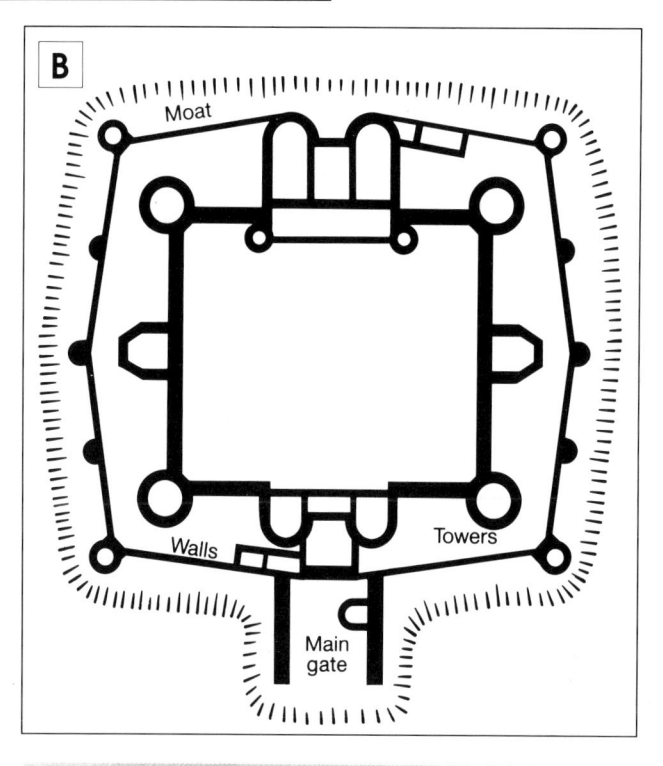

A

(map showing sea, cliffs, river, ravine, ford, with 0–100 metres scale)

B

(plan of castle showing moat, walls, towers, main gate)

C

(illustration of the castle)

Look at map **A**. It shows a site Edward I chose for one of his castles in Wales. He gave orders to his chief castle builder, Master James of St George, to plan out the castle. Master James built the castle along the latest, most advanced lines of the 1280s. This meant that the castle was made up of rings of defences, so that if an enemy broke through one ring they would face the next. We call such castles **concentric** because the rings of defences have a central point.

Edward I built eight concentric castles in Wales. Beaumaris, on Anglesey, is a stunning example of a concentric castle. It is one of the most amazing sites I have ever visited. **B** shows its plan, **C** what Alan Sorrell thinks it might have looked like. A castle like Beaumaris could hold out until the last tower was taken. You can work out from **B** and **C** what might have been in Master James' mind when he planned the castle.

Can you think how such castles were built? Think of the steps involved. Master James would most likely draw a plan on **parchment** (dried skin for writing on). We have such plans for monasteries and cathedrals. Then, with ropes and pegs, his men would mark out the plan on the ground. To build the castle Master James used a small army of men,

2500-3000 in all, ranging from skilled masons, carpenters and smiths down to gangs of unskilled workers who dug the foundations and the moat. All these workers had to be housed and fed. The size of the job was rather like building a modern motorway.

There were huge problems in getting the vast amounts of stone and timber to the castle on time. To build the walls Master James had wooden scaffolding, and used pulleys and winches to haul the stone up to the tops of the walls and towers, **D**.

The building season lasted from April to November, and each castle took from five to seven years to finish. We know about the building of the castles because the accounts (money paid out) survive. Do you think that this is evidence we can trust?

Castle Builder!

How well would you have done as Master James' assistant in building the castle on Site **A**? Keep a diary of your thoughts on the planning and building of the castle, see **a-d** for guidance.

a Using the Sources (AT3).
1 Look at **B** and **C**. For each of the features on **B** discuss what you think they were used for. Then think of which features you would have in your own castle.
2 Look at **D**. For each of the builders, suggest what job they are doing and why.

b Planning your Castle (AT1).
Your castle will have all the features below. You might find it easiest to cut out counters for each of the features. You can then move them around the site, working out the best place for them.

- A deep moat around the castle
- A dock which will be built into the castle
- A drawbridge from the dock to one of the castle entrances, either the main entrance or a tower/pair of towers.
- Towers - the castle's main defences will consist of towers, with linking walls in between. There are two types of tower, large and small. You can choose them in the following ratio:

Large	4	5	6	7
Small	16	12	8	4

The towers should be no more than 30 metres apart, a deadly distance for shooting arrows.

- Walls - these should link up the towers. Along the wall should be a parapet, and slits for firing arrows.
- A great hall, where the castle commander and up to 30 men would sleep.
- An armoury
- Kitchens
- A chapel
- Dungeons and torture chambers
- A well

c Timetable (AT1). Work out the order in which you will build your castle. Think of the workers and supplies you will need, and how you can get hold of them.

d Orders (AT1). Draw the plan of your castle, and the orders which you will send out, in the king's name, for its building.

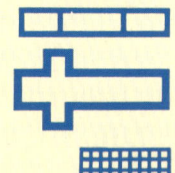

Owain Glyndwr

'Terrorist' or 'Freedom Fighter' are names you might use for the same person. It depends on whether you do or don't believe in what that person is fighting for. In Britain we have the IRA who shoot and blow up their English enemies. 600 years ago the English government faced a far worse threat than the IRA - the Welsh under Owain Glyndwr. Our best source about Owain is Adam of Usk, a Welshman who lived at the time and wrote down what he knew about Owain, **A**.

> *1401 In autumn Owain Glyndwr, with all North Wales, Cardigan and Powis as his allies, put to death by sword those English who lived there and burned their towns, in particular Welshpool.*
>
> *1402 On the day of Saint Alban [22nd June], near to Knighton in Wales a hard fought battle took place between the English... and the Welsh, with an awful killing of about 8,000 souls. The victory was with Owain... Backed by a following of thirty thousand men who streamed out of their lairs, throughout Wales and its borders Owain captured castles, amongst which were Usk, Caerleon and Newport, and fired the towns... In this year the king, with one hundred thousand men and more split up into three armies, invaded Wales to make war on Owain. But he and his poor wretches stayed in their caves and woods. So, the king burned and plundered the land and went home with countless stolen cattle.* **(A)**

(Adam of Usk)

A bloody war broke out and lasted until at last English troops beat Owain's troops and made sure Wales was back in an iron grip. Owain vanishes from the pages of History - we do not know what happened to him. **B** is a statue of him in Cardiff City Hall. In Wales Owain is still a hero. Can you think why?

Owain Glyndwr - Terrorist or Freedom Fighter?

You can use source **A** to draw a poster which either shows Owain as a 'freedom fighter' or as a 'terrorist'.

a Using your sources (AT3).
1 Use what you know from pages 46-48 to help you.
2 Work out from source **A** which areas of Wales Owain conquered, and the places he burned.

b Your ideas (AT2).
1 Think with care about how you will use the evidence from source **A** to paint Owain as a terrorist or as a freedom fighter.
2 Go through it and pick out the details which you would use either to attack or to defend Owain.

c The Poster (AT1, AT2).
Think of how you might put your ideas down on a poster - you want to get across as clear a view of him as you can. Put your posters up as a wall display and look at how different pupils have used the same evidence in different ways. How does the statue **(B)** portray Owain as a hero?

Edward I and Scotland

What do Scottish claims to be free from English rule suggest about the way Scots think of themselves? Scottish pride in their country, nationalism, goes back a long way. A key period in Scotland's history was the Scottish fight to free themselves of English rule during the reigns of Kings Edward I and Edward II (1307-27). A turning point was the Battle of Bannockburn (1314), when the Scots smashed an English army (see page 54).

Scotland is a country of hills, mountains, rivers, lakes and rich low-lying land. In the 1300s, lowland Scottish lords and knights ruled their estates in the same feudal way as lords and knights did in England - see page 22. In the mountains the Scots lived in tribes or clans, each with its own clan chief. Scotland's kings had a hard and thankless task in ruling the country. The Scottish nobles - the feudal lords and the clan chiefs - were always fighting each other, and the Scottish king. A French visitor later wrote about how the Scots went to war:

These Scots are very tough indeed because of their constant wearing of arms and fighting. When they enter England they will in a single day and night travel 24 miles; for they ride on sturdy horse and bring no wagons with them. **(A)**

When I read Adam of Usk's Chronicle (see page 46), I found a piece which told me why the Scots were such tough enemies:

The Scots, when they fled to places to hide, laid waste and stripped their fields and houses and farms, to stop them supplying our king. They lurked in thick forest and the hiding places of secret caves and woods... Yet they did often come out from these lairs, and in lonely deserts and cut-off places they slew and took very many of our men prisoner, doing us more harm than them. **(B)**

Do you know what we call this kind of warfare today?

What was the Scottish struggle against the English about?

The timeline will help you work out what went on.

TIMELINE

1290 • The heir to the Scottish throne, the Maid of Norway, was due to marry Edward I's son, but she died.
• After the Maid's death, two great Scottish lords, John Balliol and Robert Bruce, claimed the throne.
• The Scots turned to Edward I to help sort out who should rule.
• The English king believed that the Scottish king should pay him homage and obey him.
• Edward backed John Balliol to be Scottish king.
1293 Balliol had a row with Edward, and wanted to be break free from Edward's control.
1294 Edward went to war with France, and Balliol seized his chance to rise against him.
1294-1314 Edward I and Edward II (1307-27) fought many campaigns in Scotland.
1307 Edward I died on campaign against the Scots. As a lucky charm his bones were carried in a bag on a pole at the front of the army, but they did the English little good. Edward II became King of England.
1314 By 1314 the Scots, under a new skilled leader, Robert Bruce, had driven English out of most of Scotland and captured nearly all of their castles.

Strategy! (AT1)

A war game can give you some idea about the kinds of problems which faced Edward I and II when they tried to conquer Scotland. You are asked to keep a diary of your campaign.

a Strategy is a game for two players. The board represents Scotland; mountain areas and castles are marked. Decide who will be the Scottish leader, Bruce, and who the English king.
b The aim of the game is to drive the other player off the map.
c Now play the game. Keep a diary of your campaign saying what your thoughts were at each move. Pick out from sources **A** and **B** points which you think you might include about how the Scots campaigned or fought.

RULES
1 Pieces - four counters for the Scots, two for the English. Counters or coins can be used as pieces.
2 Place the Scottish pieces in C3, the English in E7. The English move first.
3 Any number of pieces can be in the same square.
4 Moves: a piece can be moved from any one square to any square next to it - they can move diagonally.
5 English pieces can move from any square on the coast to any other coast square, eg E2 to F6. Scottish pieces CANNOT move in this way.
6 English pieces CANNOT move into mountain squares - Scottish pieces CAN.
7 After three rounds the Scots gain ONE extra piece, in C3, and an EXTRA piece for each three following rounds, all in C3.
8 After five rounds the English gain ONE extra piece, in E7, and an EXTRA piece every five rounds in that square.
9 For each round write down the moves of the pieces. Each piece moves separately.
10 You can have more than one of your pieces in a square.
11 CAPTURES TABLE
The table shows how pieces in the same square can capture each other or a castle.

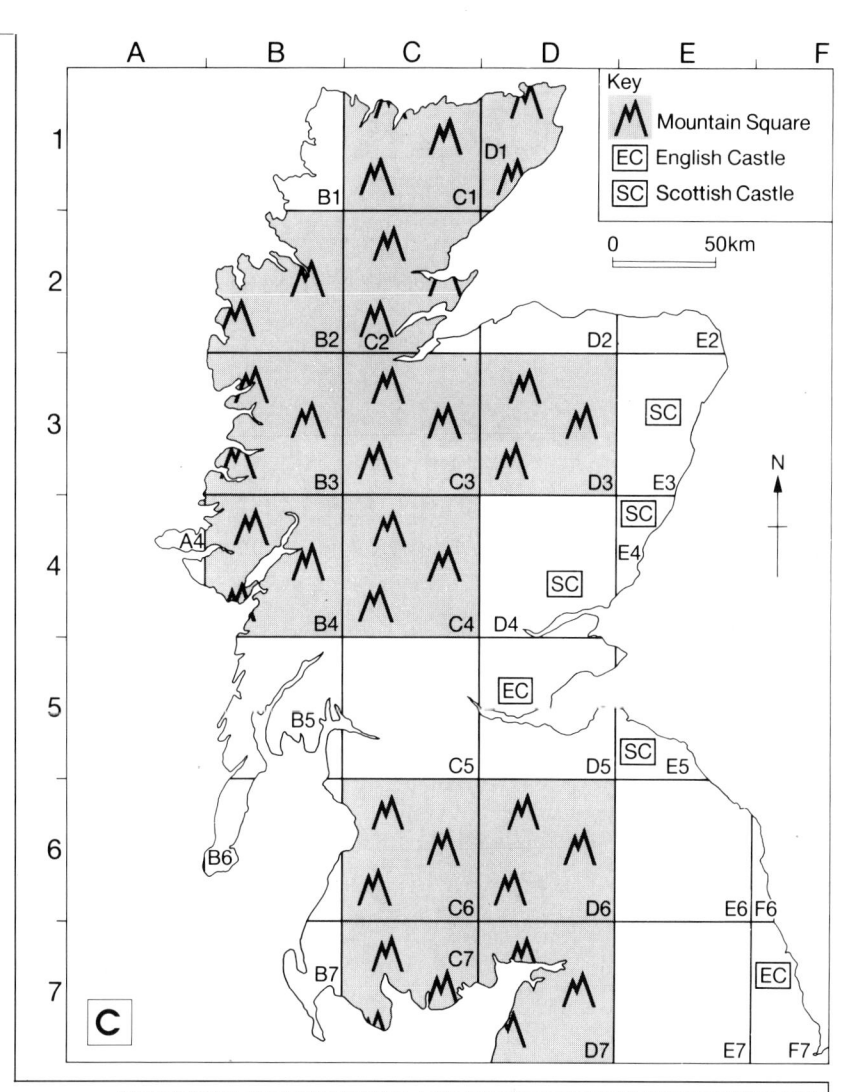

CAPTURES TABLE			
Type of square	Scottish counters	English counters	Result
EC	3 or more	0	Scots gain castle
EC	3 or more	1 or more	Scots lose 2 counters
EC	2 or less	0 or more	Scots lose 2 counters
SC	1 or more	1 or more	English lose 1 counter
SC	0	1 or more	English gain castle
Open	1	2	Scots lose 1 counter
Open	1	1	English lose 1 counter
Open	2	2	Scots lose 1 counter
Open	3	1 or 2	English lose 1 counter
Open	4 or more	2	English lose 2 counters
Open	4 or more	3 or more	Scots lose 1 counter English lose 3 counters

Bannockburn

When you go on a school trip, you are often given a leaflet, worksheet or guide to a building or battlefield. We will ask you to produce such a guide for the battle of Bannockburn.

What was the battle about? In 1314 Edward II of England marched with his army of about 3000 knights and 15000 footsoldiers to crush the Scots. The Scots had attacked the last English castle in Scotland at Stirling, **A**. If Stirling fell, Robert Bruce would sweep the English out of Scotland. At Bannockburn Edward II came face to face with Robert Bruce's army, less than half the size of his own force.

Bruce had worked out a new way of fighting against the heavy English armoured knights, the tanks of their day. Bruce armed his men with long pikes, **B**, and massed them together in a **schiltron.** From the distance a schiltron looked like a giant hedgehog. The schiltron was a deadly weapon, horsemen who dashed against it ended up looking like a pin cushion. At Bannockburn the schiltron faced its hardest test.

How did the battle go? The plan, **C**, shows the armies drawn up ready to fight, with the

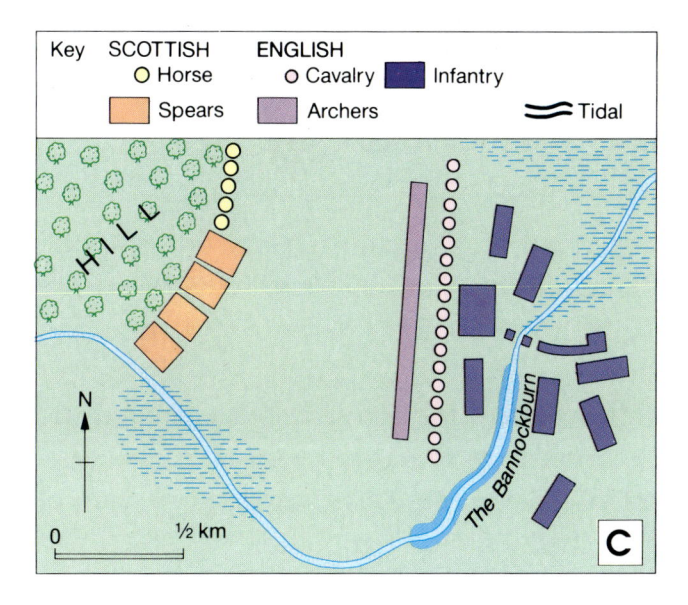

Key
SCOTTISH: ○ Horse, ☐ Spears
ENGLISH: ○ Cavalry, ■ Infantry, ▬ Archers, ≈ Tidal

English at the bottom of the hill. The Scottish schiltrons would have to stand firm against an uphill charge of the English knights on horseback, **B**. What else suggests that this was not the best place for knights to fight? Edward ordered his horsemen to attack the Scots, but they faced a dense wall of spears and were forced back. As the English retreated the Scots pushed down the hill. The English knights became tangled up in the forces behind them; think of the chaos, confusion, swearing, shouting, panic and fear.

On three sides marsh, brook and ravine hemmed in Edward's men, on the fourth the deadly Scots drove the English back.

The slaughter was horrific. The English troops in blind panic tried to flee across the mud and marsh of the Bannockburn. Weighed down with their heavy armour the English horses, knights and footsoldiers became stuck. The tide came in and drowned those the Scots had not killed or captured. A Scot wrote of the English disaster:

> **❝** Many nobles were killed, a great many were drowned in the waters and slaughtered in the pitfalls. Many died in all sorts of ways and many - a great many - nobles were captured. **❞** (**D**)
>
> (Anon)

The Bannockburn Story

As if you were either a Scottish or an English nationalist prepare a background story on the Battle of Bannockburn for a children's guide to the battle. You could do this as a set of cartoons showing key events, a datechart with key facts on it, a drawing of the fighting, or a simple children's story or poem from the viewpoint of a Scottish or English soldier.

a Studying the sources (AT3).
Use the text, sources **A-D** and what you can find in other books to sort out what happened and when:
- the key facts
- where and when the campaign took place
- the characters involved
- what the soldiers looked like - how they fought
- how the battle went.

b Creating the guide (AT2). Work out how you can best get your ideas across. Each cartoon will need a title, the story or poem will have to tell the tale from the viewpoint of a Scot or an Englishman, the drawing will have to show in detail how the two sides fought.

Use these words and ideas to help: night, camp, smith's workshop, wake up, breakfast, tell stories, rumours, orders, march, draw up, enemy, wait, sounds, smells, feelings, archers, arrows, charge, pikes, swords, horses, screams, neighs, bodies, blood, panic, marsh/tide/mud, slaughter.

c Comparing the guides (AT2).
When you have finished, compare your guides. What differences are there between the Scottish and the English 'versions'? Why?

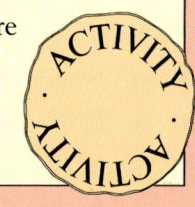

ACTIVITY

The battle meant that the Scots had won their freedom from the English. No English king ruled Scotland for the rest of the Middle Ages. Today the Scots still regard Bannockburn as a triumph against a deadly enemy.

The Medieval Village

What did your home or school area look like in the Middle Ages? You can find out by hunting out clues from the past and using your imagination to build up a picture in your mind of the medieval countryside. Many clues survive from medieval times, like old buildings, ruins, field boundaries, roads and place names and written clues such as the Domesday Book.

Look out of the window and think of what you might see if there were no buildings, roads, electric and telephone wires. Instead there is grassland, forest, shrub, marsh, hill or mountain. What was England like in 1086? Britain's most famous landscape historian wrote source **A**, which paints a great picture of the English landscape at the time of the Domesday Book, see pages 20-21.

> *Nearly every village we know today had appeared on the scene by 1086… but here and there in the still densely [thickly] wooded districts of England a few villages had to wait for their foundation until the twelfth or thirteenth century… Around nearly every village stretched its open fields, either two or three in number, each covering a few hundred acres, but hardly anywhere had these fields reached the frontiers of the village territory. If one walked half a mile, a mile at the most, out from the village, one came to the edge of the wild, to a wide stretch of moory or boggy ground that formed a temporary [short-lived] barrier, or the massed tree-trunks of the primeval [ancient] woods still awaiting the axe. Every village had its own frontiers… perhaps half of the village territory…still remained to be rescued from the natural wilderness.* **(A)**

(W G Hoskins 1955, The making of the English Landscape)

Where medieval men and women lived depended on the countryside. So, on wild, bleak granite moorland you would find the odd, lonely sheep farm huddling in a sheltered spot. But, in rich, low-lying river valleys where the forest had been felled the peasants' huts would be grouped in a village, often as large as a small town, at the hub of up to half a dozen open fields.

By 1066 the peasants would have chopped or burned down large amounts of woodland to make new or larger fields for growing wheat or barley, or to raise sheep and cattle. Medieval people cleared huge areas of forests in the same way as the rain forests are now being chopped down in Africa and South America. What do you think this did to the soil? Map **B** shows how a local historian thinks the place where I used to live looked 700 years ago. Compare the map with what Hoskins wrote in source **A**.

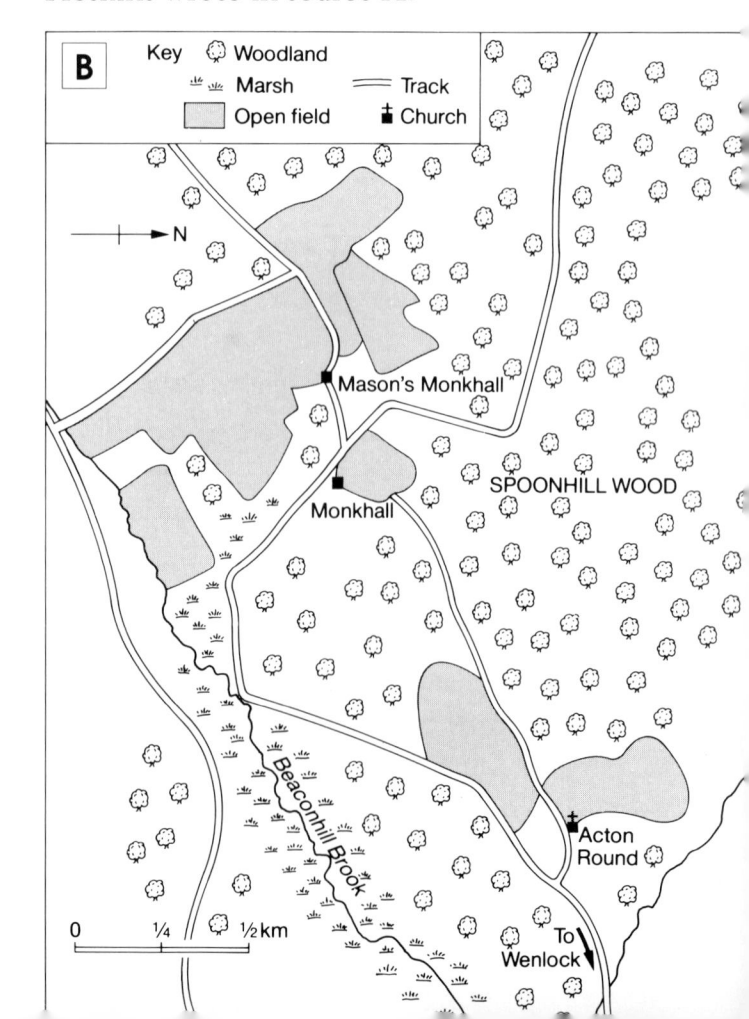

What was a large medieval village like? **C** is a plan of Newton, based on a large village near Cambridge. In the village live people drawn from real life, Rainald the Lord, Eleanor his wife, Odo the reeve, Orderic the priest and lots of villagers. We will meet all these people on pages 58-67.

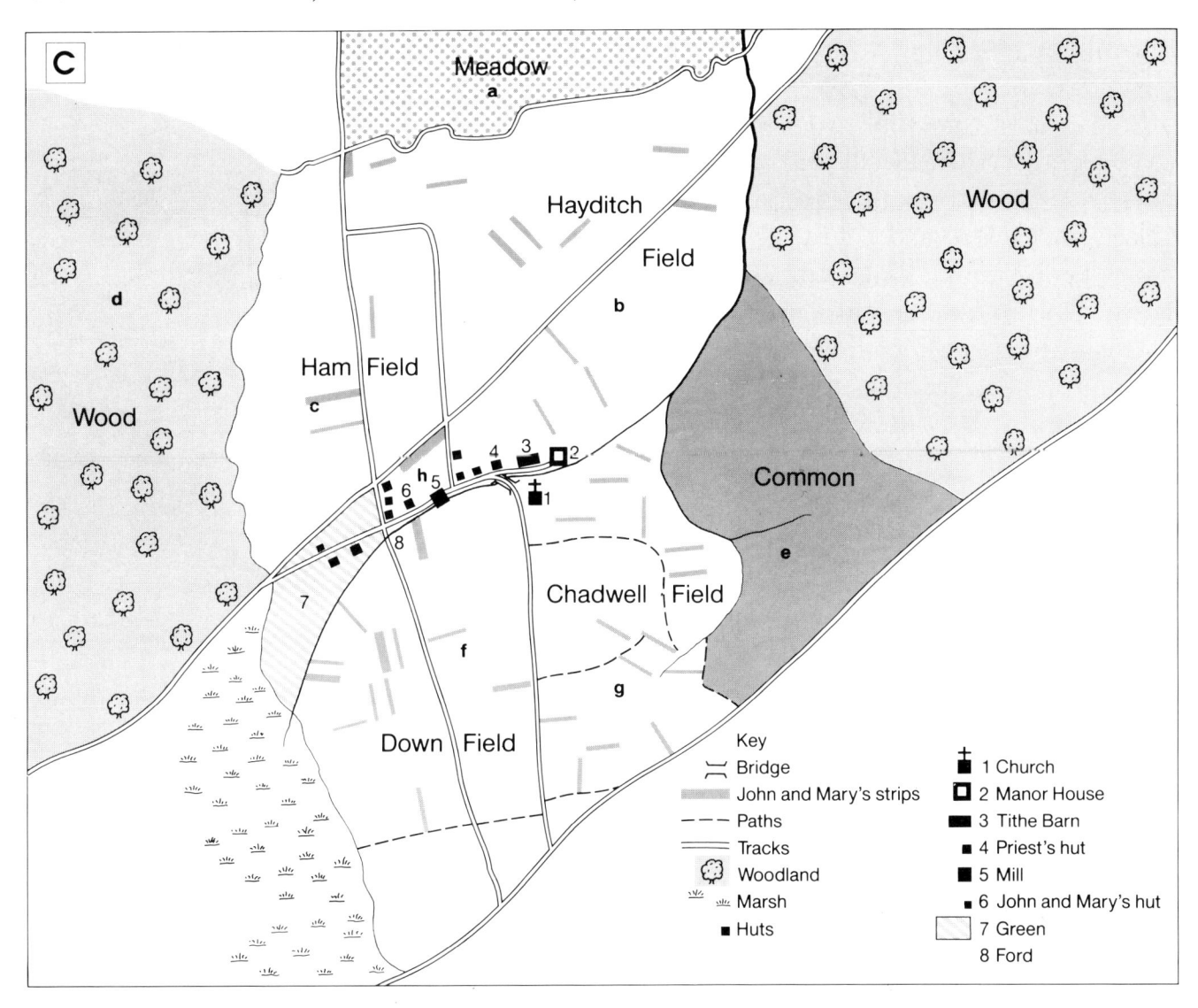

C — Plan of Newton village

Key:
- Bridge
- John and Mary's strips
- Paths
- Tracks
- Woodland
- Marsh
- Huts
- 1 Church
- 2 Manor House
- 3 Tithe Barn
- 4 Priest's hut
- 5 Mill
- 6 John and Mary's hut
- 7 Green
- 8 Ford

Labelled areas: Meadow (a), Hayditch Field (b), Ham Field (c), Wood (d), Common (e), Chadwell Field, Down Field (f, g), Wood.

Local Historian - The Medieval Village

To learn about your own area you have to think like a local historian. We know about the Cambridge village, **C**, because of a famous book about it, *The Common Stream*, which Rowland Parker wrote. He worked out what his village was like using place-names, local history books, old maps, entries in Domesday Book and the present parish boundaries. We would like you to work in the same way to discover how your own area might have appeared in medieval times.

Handling sources (AT3)

1 What might your area have been like? Use **B** to think about it. Describe what you might have seen on a walk along a track from west to east and north to south.

2 What might a local village's lands and buildings have been used for? Look at **C** and say what you can see at points **a** to **h**. Draw up a list of features and their uses, taking a village near your home or school as an example:

Village Name.............................	
Feature	Uses
1	
2 etc	

Now describe what you might have seen on a walk through points **a** to **h** on one of
- a spring day
- a summer day
- an autumn day
- a winter day.

ACTIVITY

The Villagers

A is the picture I like most from medieval History. Can you guess why? What single word or phrase comes into your mind when you look at it? Although all peasants like the one in A worked on the land, in a large village like Newton many of them would also have special jobs. A peasant could be a smith, leather worker, carpenter, weaver, potter miller, or the village inn keeper! Women as well as men could learn the village's crafts. B-D show what village life might have been like.

The peasants made up one huge family of mums and dads, aunts and uncles, cousins and grandparents. Families were large, but young - few people lived beyond forty. Life was nasty, brutish and short. Disease struck down babies and young chidren, for there were no modern medicines, doctors, nurses and hospitals. In times of bad weather and crop disease the peasants would go hungry or even starve to death.

The Anglo-Saxon Chronicle has many entries about famine. I think E is one of the most striking:

66 *In this same year over the whole of England, disease among cattle and pigs was worse than any within living memory; so that in a village where ten or twelve ploughs were in use, not a single one was left working; and a man who owned two or three hundred pigs found himself with none. After that the hens died, and then meat and cheese and butter were very scarce. May God improve matters when it is his will!* 99 (E)

(The Anglo-Saxon Chronicle 1131)

Medieval Happy Families

Design a set of four playing cards for one of the trades in the village, Table **F**.
A set of four cards should show a craftsman or woman, the raw materials they use, their tools, and what they make. Each card should have the craft written at the top.

a Making the cards (AT1, AT3). Make a set of cards by yourself, as a pair or as a group activity. Split the work up among the whole class, so each family of cards is covered.
1 To make cards, fold a sheet of A4 paper into eight, with four oblongs for each set of playing cards.
2 Each row in Table **F** suggests the pictures for a family of four cards. I have left some gaps. Work out what should go in these gaps, using **A-D**. Copy and complete the table.
3 Discuss what extra family cards you can add to the pack, and design them. Do this on paper or card the same size as the cards for Table **F**.
4 Cut out your completed set of cards, and play the game. The rules are simple. Shuffle the cards - give each player five cards. Place the remainder face down. On each player's turn they can take one card from the pack and discard one card to put on the pack's bottom. The winner is the player who gets a complete family set first.

b Story (AT1). Write a story of a day in the life of the village. Write about the things you see, what the peasants might tell you about their work, and how they live.

ACTIVITY ACTIVITY

F	CRAFTSMAN	RAW MATERIAL	TOOLS	WHAT MADE
	Mason John Rogers	Mason picture of stone	Mason ?	Mason ?
	Miller Joan Skep	Miller ?	Miller picture of mill	Miller ?
	Leatherworker Peter Lee	Leatherworker draw hides	Leatherworker draw tools	? ?
	Carpenter John Lawe	Carpenter ?	Carpenter ?	? ?
	Smith June Everard	Smith draw raw materials	Smith ?	Smith ?
	Brewer/ Innkeeper Margaret Robberts	Brewer/ Innkeeper ?	Brewer/ Innkeeper ?	Brewer/ Innkeeper ?
	Potter Mary Spenser	Potter ?	Potter picture of wheel	Potter ?
	Weaver Eve Waugh	Weaver ?	Weaver ?	Weaver ?

D

The Village Economy

John and Mary Fuller spent their lives as peasants working in the fields of Newton. Like most people in medieval England they lived in a village or hamlet, for towns were few and tiny, see page 68. THINKING HISTORY means that you have to ask questions - what questions would you add to list **A** about John and Mary's village? You can use the same questions to find out about your own local medieval villages and hamlets.

> Table A
> 1 What did the villagers grow in the fields?
> 2 What raw materials did they get from the woods, soil, marsh and stream?
> 3 What power did they use in their work?
> 4 What animals and birds did they rear or trap?
> 5 What tools did they need?
> 6 What did they make from their raw materials?
> 7 What did they do with their goods or produce?

What a lot of things to think about!

B and **C** are two of my favourite pictures about medieval village life. They contain clues about how peasants like John and Mary lived and worked. Table **E** helps you think about how the people of Newton made a living. The medieval village had to rely on what its people could grow or make. There was little trade, people could only travel on foot or horseback along rough tracks, and visits to the local town market were rare.

John and Mary Fuller's family grew the food they needed - rye, wheat, beans and peas on their 40 strips of land. The strips were spread around the village's four open fields - see page 62. The Fullers also had a share of the village's hay harvest from the meadow, and their cows, oxen, sheep and horse grazed on the common along with Rainald's war horse. When the Fullers killed an animal or bird, almost every bit was eaten or used as raw materials, see table **E**.

Mary Fuller would dry, pickle or salt down any meat they could not eat straight away for winter. Each year a different crop would be grown in the common fields, while one was left fallow (rested). For that year the village animals would mainly graze on the lord's strips in the fallow field, enriching his soil with their dung.

The Fullers slaved away all year to make a living. An interview with a woman farm worker 500 years later, **D**, gave me an insight into Mary's life. Little would have changed.

The Village Economy

As a local historian you can work out what the medieval village economy might have been like for hamlets or villages near your home or school.

a Studying the sources (AT3).
1 Look at pictures **B** and **C** for 30 seconds.
2 Write down or talk about three things you can see in each, and what ideas and feelings the pictures give you.
3 For each picture say who the people in them are and what they are doing.
4 Use table **E** to say which part of the village the pictures might show.
b The Village (AT1)
1 For each part of the village in Table **E** jot down ideas about what might be going on on a summer day. **D** gives some clues.
2 You can draw a picture of ONE village scene for one part of the village. Try to share out the parts of the village so that you get a complete class set of pictures of village scenes, which you can talk about and put up as a display.
3 Copy out Table **E** and add a final column which says which villagers made each product.
c Tools (AT3). Work out what tools John and Mary would need for the following: •digging ditches; •sifting grain and chaff; •carrying milk and water; •threshing corn; •weeding; •trimming hedges; •hooking thorns; •cutting corn; •cutting grass and hay in the meadow. Draw up a similar list of tools and implements, and their uses, which Mary also used in the house.
d The Village Economy (AT1).
Now copy out my list of questions in Table **A** with your answers to them.

ACTIVITY

66 *I got up as early as half-past two, three, four, or five, to get cows in, feed them, milk them and look after the pigs. I then had breakfast, and afterwards went in to the fields. In the fields I used to drive the plough, pick stones, weed, pull turnips, when snow was lying about, sow corn, dig potatoes, hoe turnips, and reap. I did everything that boys did.* 99 (**D**)

(W G Hoskins 1966, Old Devon)

E AREA	ANIMAL, BIRD, CROP, VEGETATION	RAW MATERIAL	PRODUCT
Open Fields	Barley, Wheat, Rye Beans and Peas	Grain Peas/ Beans	Bread, Beer Vegetable Stew
Common	Sheep	Meat Wool	Mutton Cloth
	Goats	Bone Milk	Combs Cheese
	Cattle	Skins Milk Fat	Shoes Cheese Grease
	Oxen	Power	Ploughing
	Hens	Eggs	Food
	Geese	Feathers	Mattresses
Woodland	Trees Bushes	Timber	Tables Houses Wood Charcoal
	Bees	Honey-comb	Wax Candles Honey
	Roots	Withies	Hurdles Baskets
	Pigs	Meat Fat	Food Tallow
River	Fish	Fish	Fish
	Wild Birds	Feather Eggs	Pillows Food
	Power	Mill	Flour
Marsh	Reeds Mud	Reeds Mud	Thatch Wattle
	Ducks	Feathers Eggs/Duck	Coats Food
	River Bank	Mud	Daub
Soil	Iron, Copper, Lead Ore	Molten metals	Tools, Pots
	Stone	Carved stone	Walls
	Clay	Bricks	Walls
	Peat	Peat blocks	Fuel

The Farming Year

How did John and Mary Fuller, and the other peasants, farm Newton village's lands? I have used what I found out from history books to make up interviews with villagers.

JON Eleanor, your husband Rainald is lord of the village. He is away at present and you are running the village. Can you tell us how you run the farm?

ELEANOR All of the village and its lands is called a manor. Rainald is Lord of the Manor. We leave Odo, our bailiff or reeve, in charge of our own strips. We have 130 strips on our demesne farm. We get Odo to tell the peasants what they have to do on the three days a week they have to work for us. The peasants also have to put in **boon work** (extra hours for their lord) at key times, such as the harvest.

JON How, John, do you and the villagers organise the farming year?

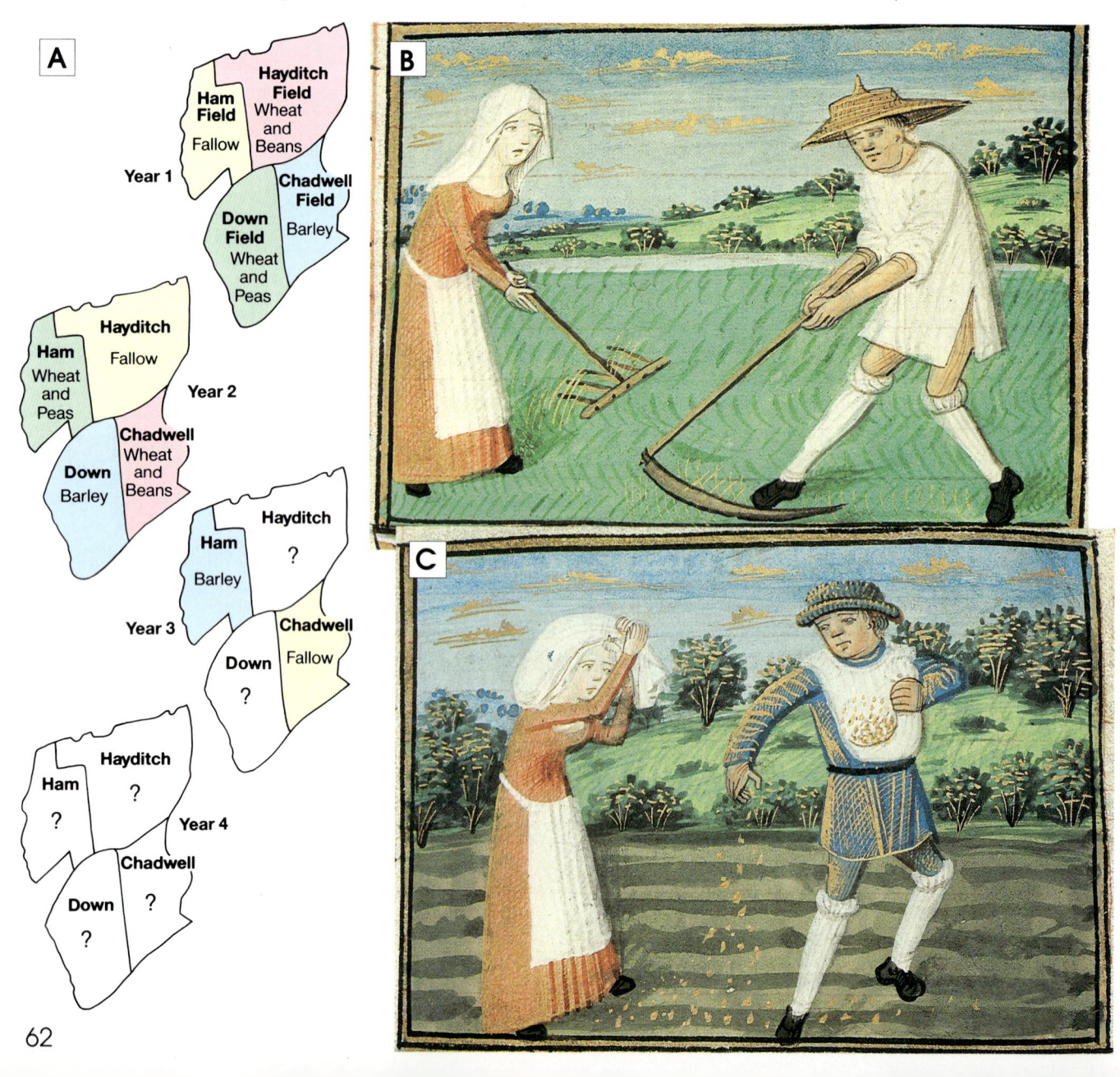

JOHN FULLER Each year we grow a different crop in three of the common fields, barley, oats, peas or beans, while the fourth field is rested or left fallow. In four years the crops go round in a circle. This is called a rotation (**A**). We all keep our cows, goats and horses on the fallow field, but they all have to live mainly on the lord's strips. The animals' muck seems to make his soil much richer.

JON Mary, what goes on each year at the village meeting?

MARY FULLER Once a year Odo calls a meeting of the peasants in the church to decide on the work to be done in the common fields, meadow and how to run the common.

JON Margaret Robberts, you run the pub and also farm 30 strips. What is a strip?

MARGARET ROBBERTS Each of the common fields is split into strips, called furlongs [a furrow long]. A furlong is about 200 metres long by about 20 metres wide - an acre [half an hectare] of land. An acre is the amount of soil I can plough in a day. 200 metres is about how far a horse walks before turning around at the strip's headland. My plough cuts a single, narrow furrow or trench in the soil (see **C**, page 60). My strips have been farmed for several hundred years. With the plough throwing up the earth to the right, can you guess what has happened to the strip? Between each strip is a balk of unploughed land. I have also got some wooden fences, called fleaks, which at times I use to cut off my strips from those of my neighbours. Can you think why?

The pictures in **B** and **C** come from a medieval calendar. I worked out Table **D** from a university History book about medieval farming. It tells you what needed to be done in the farming year.

D	What needed to be done in...	
Month	the fallow field	farmed fields, meadow and the woods
January		carry out and spread manure
February		ditching, fencing, lambing time for sheep
March		ploughing (plough in manure and old straw from cowstalls)
April	First deep ploughing	harrow the field to prepare ground for sowing, sow oats and barley
May		scythe grass to make hay, weed crops
June	Second ploughing shallow - to kill weeds and thistles	weeding, tear up thistles by roots, pick hemp and flax, leave to dry to make rope and linen
July		weeding, scare away birds
August		harvest, reaping and threshing wheat, rye and barley
September		threshing, odd jobs
October	Final deep ploughing	deep ploughing, slaughter animals
November		threshing, hedging, ditching, cut timber
December		odd jobs, make hurdles

Medieval Calendar (AT1, AT3)

You can design a medieval calendar. Split up the twelve months among you. You can do more than one. The best twelve pictures can be a wall display which shows what happens throughout the year.

1 Look at **B** and **C** and decide which month each picture shows and what the peasants are doing (AT3).
2 Then, using the text and Table **D**, make out a list like the one below to show what you might put in a calendar picture for each month of the year.
3 Include in your list the orders which Odo might give to the peasants working on the lord's demesne.

Month   Your Calendar Picture

January...
....
Odo's Orders...
....

and so on for the next eleven months. Design your picture or describe in detail what your picture would show.

Rainald, Lord of the Manor

A

Panic - news has arrived that a band of soldiers is marching to attack Newton, burning, killing and stealing on their way. Rainald and his wife Eleanor rush to the Motte and Bailey, (see page 18). With their reeve Odo they check that the walls are strong, the ditch clear of fallen branches, the well clean, the granary full of grain and the armoury stocked with poleaxes, spears, swords, bows and arrows.

Rainald rides to the meadow to practise fighting, charging with lance and sword play, **A**. Meanwhile, Eleanor takes part in archery practice. Odo gets the peasants to drive their animals into the Bailey, and makes sure that the men are armed and ready with spears, shields and bows and arrows.

The news of the enemy attack proves to be a false alarm. The panic is over. After lunch Rainald and Eleanor go hawking, **B**. Then they sit as judges at a meeting of the Manor Court. 12 of the richer peasants form a jury to try the cases.

The Manor Court. Rainald and Eleanor keep an iron grip on the village through the Manor Court. John and Mary Fuller and the other peasants do not only have to work for Rainald. The peasants also have to pay money called **fines** for almost everything they do. They have to pay their Lord to get married, to fence in common land, and to buy strips from other families. They have to pay fines if they break local laws like:

> *No peasant shall allow his ducks or geese to be or go in the common brook running through the middle of the village... on pain of a fine of 3s 4d. for each offence.* (C)

(Foxton Court Roll)

64

Cases and fines are written down on the Manor Court's Court Roll. Court Rolls give us an amazing insight into medieval life, as the extracts in **D** show. The original names have been changed to those of Newton peasants.

> **1** *John Rogers' horses are daily in the cornfields of the peasants, and is fined 20 d.*
> **2** *Orderic, the parson of the Church, is in mercy for his cow caught in the lord's meadow.*
> **3** *Orderic, John Fuller, Peter Lee, John Law, June Everard and Margaret Robberts played illegal games.*
> **4** *It is likewise ordered that John Fuller…clean out the common brook from the house of Eve Waugh to the mill of Joan Skep, on pain of a fine of 6s 8d.*
> **5** *From June Everard 6d for the wound she gave Mark Waugh.*
> **6** *Peter Lee gives 2s for being married with licence.*
> **7** *John Rogers' son by night invaded the house of Peter Lee and in felony threw stones at his door so that the said Peter raised the hue. Fine - 2s (one shillings=5p. 2.4d=1p)* **(D)**

When Rainald is away Eleanor takes over the running of the village. Rainald often has to go and do castle watch or fight for his overlord Judhael.

The Manor Court

You can hold a manor court to try cases in the village. You choose a jury of 12 peasants. Two or three of you can represent each peasant. First, the court has to sort out what the local laws are.

a Sorting out the Evidence (AT3).
1 Read through each of the cases, 1-7 in Source **D**.
2 Work out what the English means, and for ONE case either write it down or tell the rest of the class.
3 Then work out what you think the law is in each case plus the fine.
4 Make out a table with two columns, headed LAW and FINE.

b Trying the cases (AT2).
The jury has the following cases to try. Compare the crimes below with the ones on the Court Rolls, **D**, and try to fix a fine which fits in with the fines in **D**.
1 John Rogers the Mason, digging stone from Rainald's land without asking permission.
2 Joan Skep the Miller, milling 40 bags of flour and not paying Rainald the tax on it.
3 Joan Lawe the carpenter, marriage of her daughter, without paying the fixed charge.
4 Mary Spenser the potter, digging a load of clay from the common land, needs to pay for permission.
5 Margaret Robberts gambling in her inn without permission, **E**.
6 John Fuller poaching fish from the lord's fish pond.

c The Gamblers (AT2)
The jury has to hear case 3 on the Court Roll, **D**. They call witnesses. Each member of the form takes the role of a peasant. Write down on a piece of paper two or three sentences with your evidence for or against the accused. Say what you saw or have heard about the case. These statements can be read out to the court, and the two sides can argue their case. The jury then makes up its mind, guilty or not, and what fine to award if guilty.

The Lady of the Manor

Rainald had risen early to go stag hunting in the forest, knowing a feast would await him on his return. If you lived as a servant in his manor house, you would learn about cooking and running the home in the same way as you do at home and in domestic science. Eleanor, Rainald's wife, was in charge of you. How might your late autumn day have gone?

6am I got up and washed in cold water. Got dressed in my tunic. Gobbled breakfast - cold black bread and water.

7am Cleared away the table. Swept out the hall. Laid fresh rushes on the floor.

9am Helped Eleanor gather vegetables from the manor house's garden for the evening feast. Eleanor talked about the recipes she would use to cook the meal. This was the one we used for cabbage.

66 *Take fair cabbages, and cut them, and pick them clean. Clean wash them, and parboil them in fair water, and then press them on a fair board. Then chop them, and cast them in a fair pot with good fresh broth, and with marrowbones, and let it boil. Then take fair grated bread, and cast there into saffron and salt. And when thou servest it, knock out the marrow of the bones, and lay the marrow two pieces or three in a dish, as seems best, and serve.* 99 **(A)**

12am Had a snack of gruel, bread and cheese.

2pm Went rabbiting with Eleanor and her daughters in the lord's rabbit warren.

3pm We got the vegetables ready for supper. Chopped the meat and plucked the chickens and ducks **(B)**. Made fresh bread. Got out the trenchers (thick plates of stale bread) for everyone to eat their food off at the feast.

4pm We put the lamb, chickens and ducks on the spit in front of the great hall fire, and began cooking them for the feast **(C)**.

5pm Prepared the hall for the feast. Put trenchers, knives and goblets on the table. Got the wine and ale ready.

6pm Lord Rainald and the hunters came home, tired and hungry. They had a stag slung across one of their horses, and they dumped it in Lady Eleanor's kitchen. The men cursed and swore while they changed out of their mud-caked clothes.

7pm The feast started. My job as a page is to wait on Lord Rainald and Lady Eleanor (**D**). I had to wait for my plate of food in the kitchen. As the grown ups ate and drank, the feast became very noisy. Lots of laughter, stories and coarse jokes.

10pm The feast finished. We cleared away the tables and everyone sat around to listen to story tellers and minstrels, **E**.

12pm Rainald and Eleanor went to their bedroom. The rest of the family cleared space on the hall floor, and slept where we could.

Remember that Eleanor helped Rainald carry out all his duties as Lord of the Manor, and when he was away, at court or at war, or if he died, she would take over his job.

Kitchen Goods
1 great brass pot
6 coarse brass pots
4 little brass pots
4 great brass pots
brass pike pans
2 ladles and 2 skimmers of brass
1 cauldron
1 'dytyn' pan of brass
1 dropping pan
1 gridiron
4 rakes
3 trivets
1 dressing knife
1 fire shovel
2 trays
3 cupboards
1 frying pan
1 slice
2 great square pots
2 square pots
1 brass sieve
1 brass mortar and
1 pestle
1 grate
1 wooden sieve or cullender
1 flesh hook
2 pot hooks
1 pair tongs
1 strainer
1 vinegar bottle

(1430 - Paston Letter) (**F**)

The Medieval Feast

Medieval banquets are great fun. How well do you think you can prepare one along medieval lines?

a Work out a menu (AT1). You can have something to start with, then a huge main course of meat, fish, fowl and vegetables, followed with pudding. Don't forget the wine and ale!

b Preparing the food (AT1). A menu is one thing, turning your meat, fish, birds, fruit and veg into something delicious is another matter. Find or make up a simple recipe for one of the types of food mentioned in the text. Try to write it in the same style as **A**.

• Choose the pots and pans you would use from list **F**.

Remember that you are cooking over a huge open fire, with a bread oven at one side.

• Plan the order in which you would cook your meal.

ACTIVITY

The Medieval Town

Most medieval towns grew in a higgledy piggledy way. Would you have guessed that there were also hundreds built from scratch? Today we would call them planned towns. Can you think why a medieval lord like Rainald might want to set up a new town? English medieval towns were small, **A**, and shrank in size after the Black Death (page 92).

A	1377	1523
London	?	60,000
York	14,500	8,000
Bristol	12,700	10,000
Coventry	9,600	7,000
Norwich	8,000	10,000
Lincoln	7,000	5,000
Salisbury	6,500	8,000
Lynn	6,400	5,300
Colchester	6,000	5,300
Boston	5,700	3,500

What were planned and unplanned medieval towns like? In many ways they were like modern towns. Most days I go to a local shop to buy things we need straight away; things like bread, butter, eggs, dog food and nappies. If I want a pair of shoes I have to go into town, and if I need something like a rare book or a special fishing rod I visit the nearest city. It was just the same in medieval times. Towns were places where goods were bought, sold and made. You would also get services like justice from the baron's court in town. The kinds of goods you could buy or sell and the services you could be offered would depend upon the area which the town served, **B**. Southampton was a typical medieval town, its traders served a huge area, **C**.

How can we find out about medieval towns? Early maps, like **D**, are a major source. If you were to visit such a town you would notice many changes from today. Everywhere you would hear the sound of bells, for nearly all the big buildings in the town were churches, whose spires and towers you could see all the time. The streets were filthy, and full of shops, stalls and traders. The town was a hotspot of crime and violence. Outside the town bodies rotted on the gallows. The head of a traitor was stuck on the maingate, and in the square were the stocks and pillory.

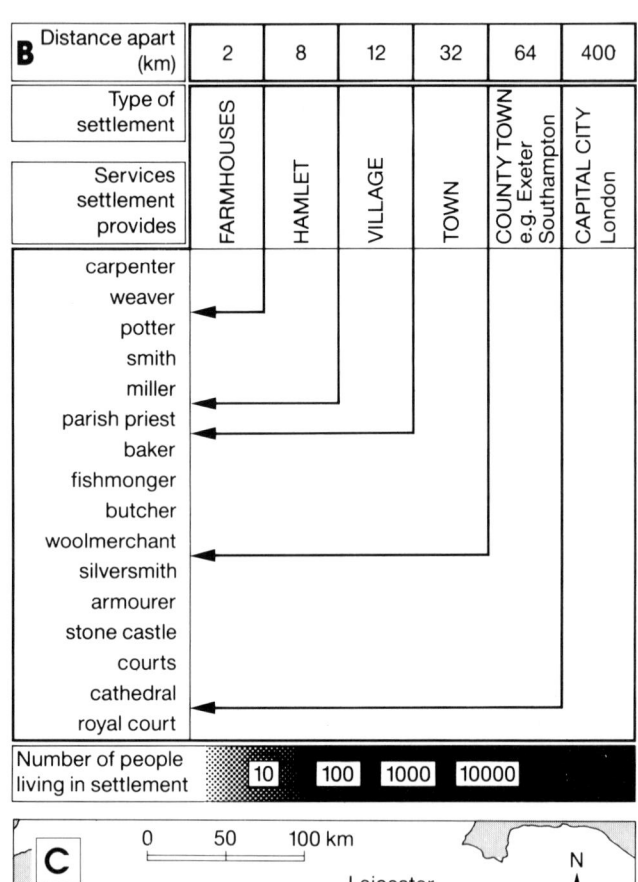

The Town Guide

You can use **D** to produce a tourist guide for Medieval Exeter. The guide will take the form of a walk through the town.

a Finding out about the Medieval Town (AT3).
1 Why did medieval towns grow up? Use **B** to see what goods and services you might get in Southampton, **C** and in your local medieval town.
2 What do the names given to Exeter's main streets (**D**) tell you about town life?
3 Why do you think Exeter's gates, walls and castle were built?

b Tourist Guide! (AT1, AT3)
1 Prepare a tourist guide for medieval Exeter, town **D** or your own local medieval town. For **D** say what you might see, smell, and hear at different points on the following route: The Key: Exe Bridge: West Gate: Butcher Row: Milk Lane: Goldsmiths Street: Gandy Lane: Rougemont Castle: East Gate: High Street: Cathedral.

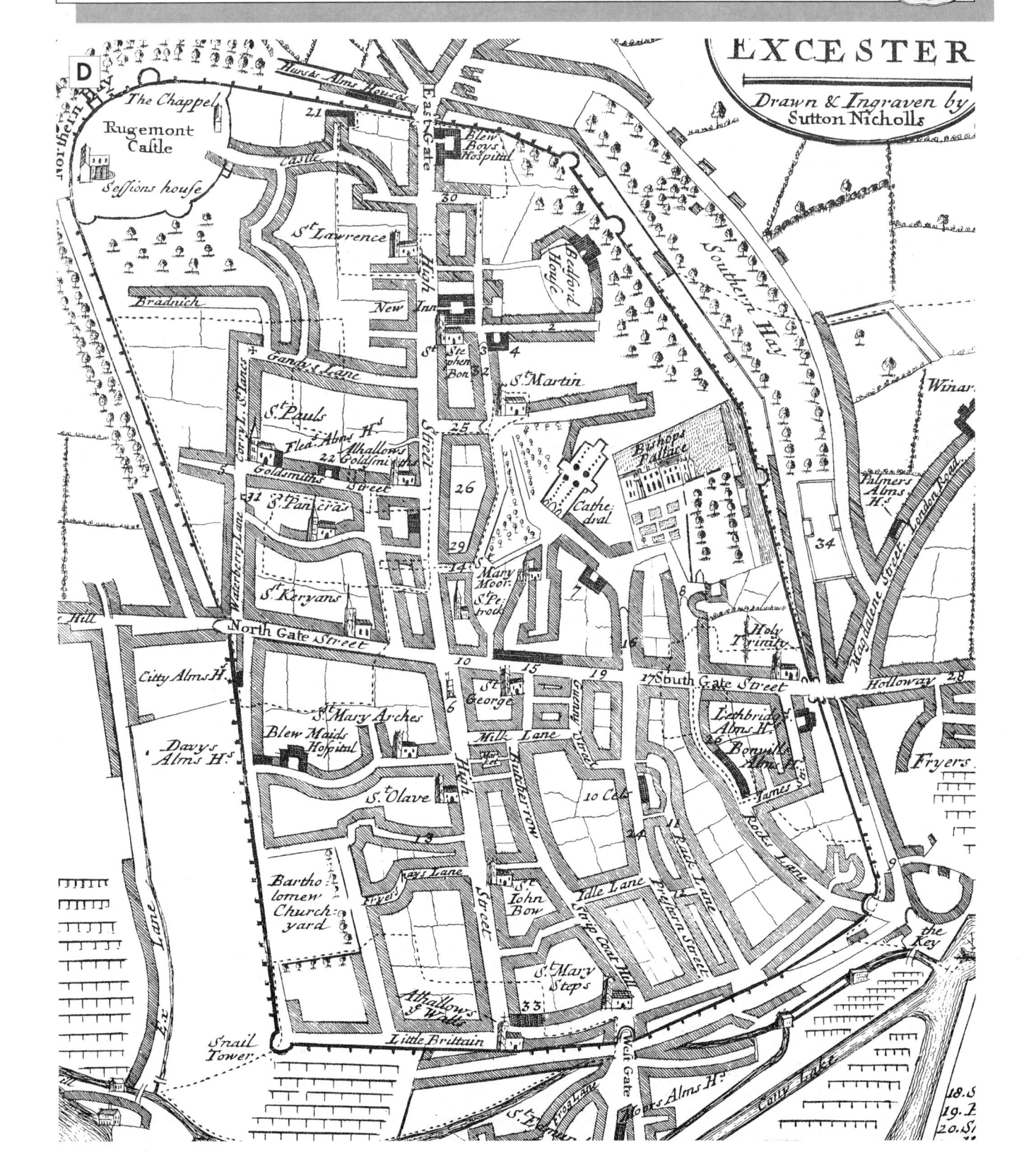

ACTIVITY

D EXCESTER
Drawn & Ingraven by Sutton Nicholls

The Town Charter

If you belong to the Guides or the Scouts you have to obey their written rules. Likewise each medieval town had its rules, laid out in its charter. The King would grant a town a charter, often in return for a huge sum of money. What kind of charter would you draw up for a new medieval planned town, and how would you run the town?

The Town's Charter and Government

1 Work by yourself or in groups. Each person or group should think about a different section of the charter. (Look at the headings below.) Each person or group should then report back their ideas about that section. Then pool your ideas to draw up a class charter.
2 The charter would be written on a special thin, scraped, cleaned and cured sheep skin called parchment - you will use paper!
3 At the top would be the charter's title, at the bottom the seals of the king, members of his council, the local lord and the town's leading traders, merchants and craftsmen, **A**. Leave space on your own charter to put in the seals.

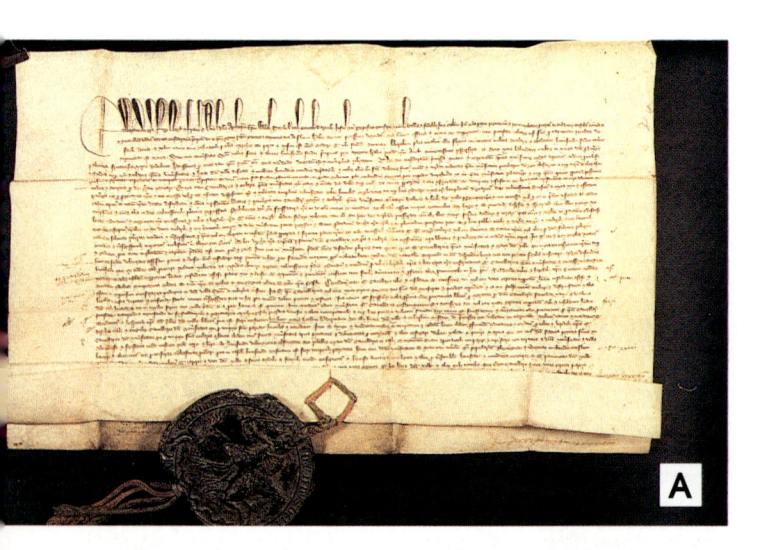

The Town's Government.

The town would have a mayor or bailiff to
• make and enforce local laws
• collect tolls and taxes
• judge cases in the local courts
• police and defend the town.

The mayor or bailiff(s) would do what the town council of aldermen told them. Aldermen made up the town council. Which of these would you would want to run your town?
1 A Mayor or two Bailiffs?
2 12, 16, 20 or 24 Aldermen?
3 Burgesses to be:
• All men who owned houses, (men only) OR
• Guild Members OR
• Men who have lived in the town for over a year.
4 Elections to be each year or every two, three or four years?
5 The town's two MPs to be chosen by the burgesses or the town council of aldermen?
6 Hold a class election to choose your mayor or bailiff(s) and town council of aldermen. Each person in the class can be a burgess.

The Town's Defences.

The council was in charge of the town's walls, gates and castle, and the people who defended them.
1 How will the castle, walls and towers be kept in good repair?
2 How will men be trained to fight to protect the town, and serve in the king's army when called upon?

Courts.

The charter allows the council to set up the town's court to try criminals and sort out rows between the people who live there.
1 When would the courts sit?
2 Who would be in charge?
3 What local laws would you make?

A

Town's Income.

The charter would allow the town council to raise money from taxes, tolls on goods being sold, rents and fines.
1 What tolls you would you get traders to pay on their goods?
2 What money you would charge for letting market stalls and for renting the town's fields?
3 What taxes would you raise?

Trade and Industry.

The council would lay down what weights and measures were to be used for selling goods. It would also make sure that things like bread and wine kept to a certain standard, and fix punishments for traders who broke the law.
1 What weights and measures would you want?
2 Decide on the punishments for traders who broke the local laws about weights and measures. Source **B** might give you some ideas.

> Cases taken from the Town court records of Salisbury
> *John Penrose sold bad and undrinkable red wine*
> *John Russell sold 37 pigeons, all bad*
> *John Strode put dust in his bread, which was full of cobwebs*
> *Alice Pegges sold loaves of bread which weighed four-fifths of an ounce too little*
> *Richard Wilton dyed his cloth with madder and woad instead of with pure woad as he claimed* (**B**)

Fire.

The Council would lay down plans for keeping fire under control. It would say who would have to keep buckets and fire hooks, and what people would have to do if a fire started. Medieval towns were mainly built from wood and straw, and went up in smoke all too often!
1 Draw up rules and orders for fighting fires
2 Act out a drama about a fire which has broken out in the shambles - the butchers' street.

The Watch.

The council would appoint a watch to make sure that the town gates were shut at night and to patrol the streets after dark. They would make sure townfolk kept to the town curfew - why would you need a curfew, to keep people in their houses after dark?
1 Draw up rules for the curfew.
2 Decide •who would man the watch •when and where it would meet •what its powers would be.
3 Choose a member of the class as a thief. Organise a hue and cry to arrest him or her.

The Streets.

Each trade would have the job of keeping the streets clean and mended in the area of its own shops and workshops. The council would also lay down laws which would tell each trade how it could carry on its affairs, such as killing sheep and cows, curing skins and brewing beer.
1 Make out orders for cleaning and mending the streets. (Think of •how often •when •who.)
2 Take one trade, and draw up rules for how it can carry on its affairs.
3 Hold a town court to try the tanners guild for letting its hides rot and for poisoning the town's water supply.

Festivals.

The Council would organise processions and town parties for major festivals.
1 Decide on which of the great religious festivals and town events you want to have a carnival and town feast for.
2 Make plans for a town procession of all the trades. (Think about •where the procession will go •the order of procession •start and finish time.)

Market Day

What was it like to be a medieval trader? The trade game helps you find out!

The Cloth Trader. The town gate is shut in your face. The gate-keeper peers out through the grille. He demands that you pay a toll for the cloth that you want to sell in the town market. You pay up. As you walk into the town the stench hits you in the face. There are piles of rotting fruit and vegetables, rubbish and dung everywhere. You step over a dead dog in the gutter. There are maggots crawling all over it. **A** was the best picture I could find to give an idea of how busy a medieval town was on market day.

The Shops. On each side of the pot-holed street are open shops. Here traders and craftsmen such as potters, weavers, silver smiths, tanners, brewers and tailors, **B**, beaver away, getting ready for the weekly market. You push your way through the shouting, jostling crowds to the central market square, where you have a cloth stall. You buy bread from the bakers, **C**.

The Market Square. At one end of the square is the poultry cross, where peasants hang their plucked hens and geese for sale, at the other end is the butter cross, piled high with fresh butter, eggs and cheese. You have to sell or swap your cloth to get the things you need.

B

C

The Trade Game (AT1, AT2)

a Background
1 This is a game to see how well you might do as a trader.
2 You are a member of a family for ONE of the trades in the list below, your teacher will tell you which one.
3 Each family must have at least two members. One person sells the goods you have made. The second person buys other goods.

b The trade tokens. Make the number of tokens shown for the trade you belong to, eg if you have eight hens, make eight tokens with a picture of a hen. The lord and lady tokens are silver groats.

Trade	Goods	Tokens	Trade	Goods	Tokens
Baker(1)	Bread	12	Baker(2)	Bread	12
Inn-keeper(1)	Beer	12	Inn-keeper(2)	Beer	12
Peasant(1)	Butter	12	Peasant(2)	Butter	12
Peasant(3)	Cheese	18	Peasant(4)	Cheese	10
Weaver	Cloth	20	Reeve	Corn	20
Peasant(5)	Hens	8	Smith	Knives	15
Butcher	Meat	14	Silver-smith	Plates	12
Potter	Pots	20	Tailor	Clothes	12
Lord	Groats	30	Lady	Groats	40

c To trade
1 You have to get one token for EACH of the goods shown.
2 You do this by swapping your goods with other people. BUT you don't have to swap one-for-one. You may be able to get more than one token of someone's goods for just one token of your own.
3 You can also swap your tokens for groats (money). How many groats is a loaf of bread worth?

d Hue and Cry. While the game goes on one of the shoppers is accused of stealing goods from one of the stalls. The town watch is called, there is an arrest. Statements are taken from witnesses. You can try the case in the town court.

e After the game
1 Write an account from the viewpoint of a medieval trader of what went on.
2 Work out a trading network, showing the links between trades using these headings •Raw Materials •What used for •Who Made it

ACTIVITY

Jobs - the Town Guilds

What job would you like to do when you leave school? In the Middle Ages you may have become an apprentice to a master of one of your local town's or city's guilds. An apprentice would learn the job by working with the master. Often he or she would live in the master's house and be like a member of the family.

A guild was a bit like a modern Trade Union. But unlike a Trade Union both the bosses (called masters) and workers (called journeymen) in a craft or trade would be members of a guild. **A** is a list of guilds in Salisbury in 1440. It shows the kinds of job that you could choose from.

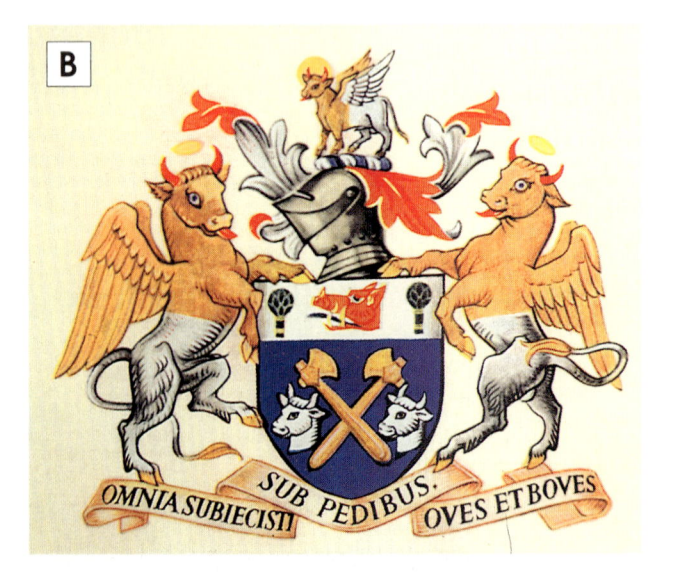

B is a guild sign - can you guess for which guild? Each guild, like a town, would have a charter to run their affairs. The charter would allow the guild to:

1 Fix prices
2 Fix the quality of the goods to be made
3 Fix the amount to be made
4 Fix the hours in the day guild members could work
5 Fix when they could sell their goods
6 Help old and ill members of the guild
7 Decide who could become a member or master of the guild
8 Set down how an apprentice should be trained during the seven years of an apprenticeship
9 Choose who should be the head of the guild
10 Have a guildhall where the guild members would meet and keep the guild records
11 Try members who had broken guild rules

Table A	
Grocers and Drapers	Goldsmiths and Blacksmiths
Weavers	Saddlers
Fullers	Pewterers
Tailors	Vintners
Brewers	Butchers and Tanners
Shoemakers	Dyers
Baker	Painters
Innkeepers	Bowmakers
Bookbinders and Parchment Makers	Glovers
Carpenters	Tilers
Builders	Arrow Makers
Barber-surgeons and Cooks	

Why do you think that traders and craftsmen ganged up into guilds, which had a complete grip on their trade in their town?

As an apprentice you would work for seven years in your master's workshop, learning all the tricks of the trade. Source **C** gives us some clues about what it was like to be an apprentice cloth dyer. After seven years you would have learned enough to become a master of the guild. To prove you were good at the job, you would be set a test. You would

C

have to make a masterpiece which the guild would judge. If it was up to scratch, you would then become a guild member after a special ceremony which would end in a huge party.

The Medieval Apprentice

To find out about getting a job today you can visit your job centre and get leaflets on hundreds of careers. Produce your own leaflet or poster about becoming an apprentice to a medieval guild. You can either produce all of the leaflet or poster yourself, or work in a group and split up the tasks, a-e among you. Choose one of the crafts in **A**.

a The Guild sign (AT3). Study **B**, and design a sign like it for your own guild.
b Studying the sources (AT3).
1 Look at **C** for 30 seconds, then cover it up and write down three things it tells you about being an apprentice dyer.
2 Find out what you can about the trade you have chosen. Include in your leaflet or poster an imaginary interview with an apprentice of the guild saying:
- where s/he works
- what her/his master is like
- what the job involves, hours, the work s/he does
- what it is like living in the master's house
- how s/he gets on with the master's wife and his sons and daughters
- how s/he spends his /her free times.

c Guild rules (AT1). Draw up a list of the guild's rules. These would include:
- who were members of the guild
- how you could become a master of the guild
- punishments for a guild member who made shoddy goods
- who could sell and make metal goods in the town
- how many guild members there could be.

d Masterpiece (AT3). Give an account of what making a masterpiece meant. Then say what the party was like, after the guild had accepted your masterpiece.

e Design (AT1). Work out a design for your leaflet or poster. Put all of your class leaflets or posters on show, and then choose which job you would most like to do.

ACTIVITY · ACTIVITY

Medieval Trade

Visit your local corner shop or supermarket. Which goods come from abroad, and where do they come from? In the Middle Ages you could also buy foreign goods, but you would have had far fewer to choose from than you have today. Can you think why? Medieval people used spices from the East to keep meat from rotting during the winter. Rich people loved to buy Italian silks and French wines. Map **A** shows that England traded all over Europe in the Middle Ages.

England's chief trade was in wool. Before 1400 England mainly sent raw wool abroad to be woven into cloth. Very little cloth was woven in England. After 1400, the wool trade changed. **B** and **C** show what happened to the wool trade. Can you work it out?

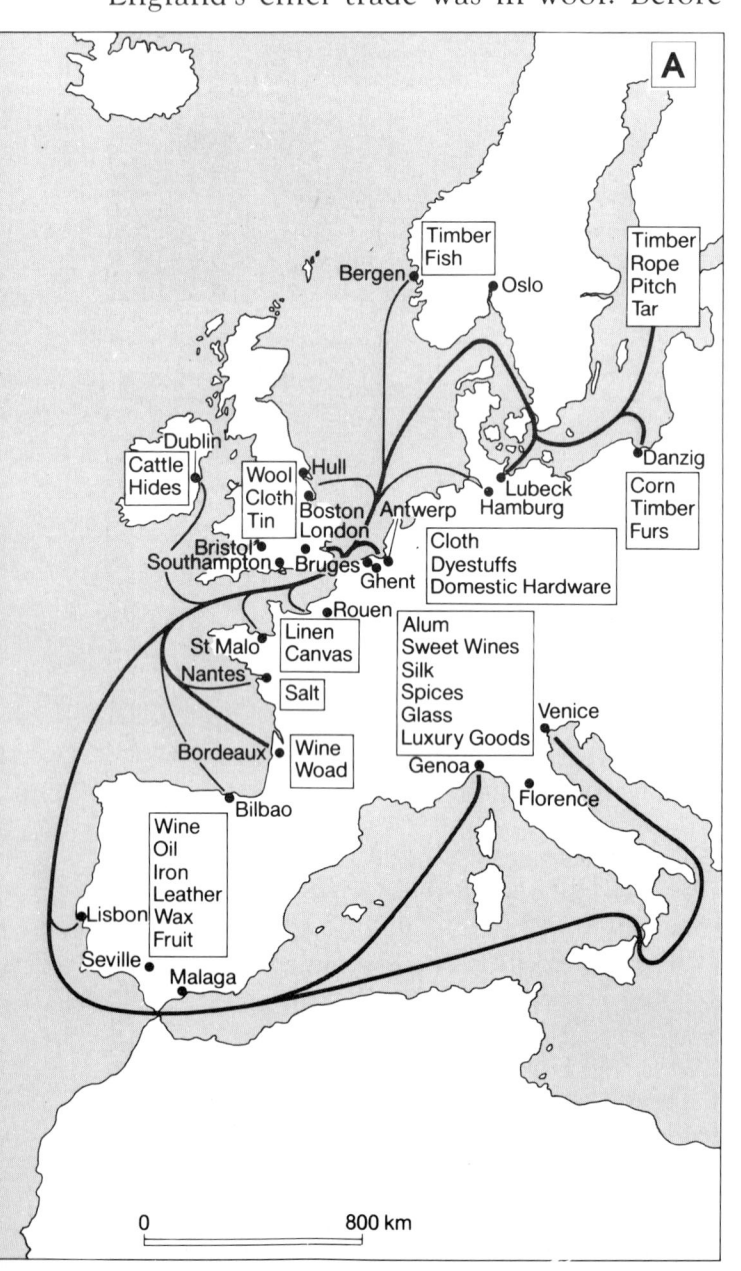

If there is a medieval church in one of your local towns or villages, you can see how much money merchants made from the wool trade. Profits from the wool trade helped to pay for these churches.

What might it have been like to be a medieval wool merchant? An historian, Alison Hanham, used the letters of a rich merchant family, called the Celys, to find out. The Celys traded in raw wool and also in sheepskins with the wool on. How did they trade?

a A merchant like William Midwinter of Northleach, Gloucestershire, would buy wool from sheep farmers to sell to the Celys.
b The Celys sent this wool to their warehouses in London or Southampton.
c The Celys then shipped this wool to Calais, in France. Calais was the port which the Government said must be used by the wool trade. It was called the Staple port, and the Celys were Staple merchants.
d At Calais the Celys sold the wool to European merchants. The Celys used this money to pay William Midwinter, and to pay the costs of running their business.

In 1486 the Celys bought their own boat, The Margaret Cely. I have used Alison Hanham's book to work out its trading trips and the profits it made (Factfile **D**). The figures are very rough. When I worked out the profits I tried to take away what the Celys must have paid for food, supplies, customs payments and wages.

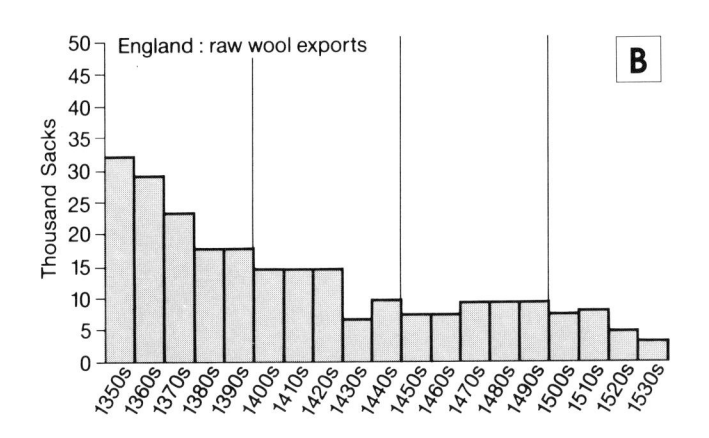

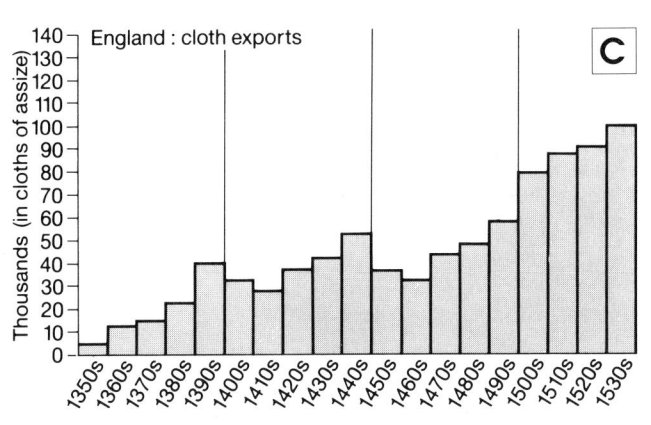

B England : raw wool exports (Thousand Sacks, 1350s–1530s)

C England : cloth exports (Thousands in cloths of assize, 1350s–1530s)

FACTFILE

D The Voyages of The Margaret Cely, 1486-7

March 1486 The Celys and a friend bought The Margaret Cely for £28. She could carry 60 tons of cargo. The ship was manned and repaired and food, drink, supplies and weapons were bought, including

> *four small serpentines (cannon)… two greater serpentines… two muskets, two hand guns, six long bows, thirty sheaf of arrows, an anchor, forty-four pellets of lead, a mould of stone to cast lead in… an horn for gunpowder.*

Sailed to London. George Cely bought a cargo of grain, cost £22.85

April 1486 Sailed to Holland (Bruges and Antwerp). Grain sold for £47.55. Ship returned to England, carrying cargo for other merchants. (Use **A** to work out what the cargo might have been.) Profit on grain, £24.70.

June 1486 Ship repaired and stocked up with food and drink, including 1,000 gallons of beer, to feed crew and soldiers. The soldiers were hired to protect the wool fleet from French attack.

July 1486 Sailed to Calais. Sale of wool cloth, minus the payments to the soldiers gave a profit of £18.80. Returned to London.

September 1486 Sailed to Bordeaux.

November 1486 - January 1487 Bought a cargo of wine. Returned to England with 55.75 tons of wine. (50 tons of this was carried for a wine merchant.) Docked in Plymouth for 11 weeks for repairs, returned to London. Profit £20.00.

The medieval merchant (AT3).

How well would you have done as a medieval merchant? Study map **A** and Factfile **D**. You have £60 to spend. On your own or with a partner, decide what to do at each point below.

1 Mark on a map where the Margaret Cely sailed in 1486-7. Mark the goods she carried.
Now think about your own voyage. Work out a list of ports you will sail to, EITHER to get pitch and tar, fish, furs, cloth OR wine, oil and leather, silk, salt.
Begin to keep a log (a diary) of your voyages.

2 You can buy a 40-ton ship (£20), or a 60-ton ship (£25). Record your choice in your log, and how much money you have left. Also write down what weapons and supplies you buy.

3 Take a cargo of wool cloth, which costs you £20. You will sell the cloth for twice what you paid for it. Which port will you sail to first?
When you arrive at your port, **toss a coin**. Heads you buy £10 of goods, tails you buy £30 of goods. Use **A** to decide what to buy, and record all your trade in your log.

4 On the way home a pirate attacks your ship. **Toss a coin**. Heads, the pirate holes your ship, and ruins half your cargo. Tails, you beat off the attack without losing any cargo. Record what happens in your log.

5 In Southampton you sell your cargo for twice what you paid for it (think about what this means if you have lost some cargo). **Toss your coin**. Heads, you sell all your cargo. Tails, you only sell half. Complete your log for the voyage. Record the profit you made on the voyage. Carry on sailing until you have traded for all the items on your list.

ACTIVITY

The Norman Church

The battle of Hastings was over and Harold's mangled and stripped body was ready to be buried. William gave thanks to God for his victory and ordered that a church should be built on the spot where Harold fell. Here priests were to pray for the souls of the dead of both sides. William was religious. He believed that God decided everyone's fate. When people died, God would send them either to heaven or to hell (**A**). It was only in the previous 140 years that the Normans had become Christians. But William strongly supported the bishops, priests, monks and nuns of Normandy in their work. Because of William's support, the Church became very important in Norman England.

The Church's bishops and priests crowned and blessed the King, held church services and married, baptised, and buried people. The Church also looked after the old and sick. Men and women left both land and money to the Church when they died, so the Church was very rich. But the Church had another role. Knights lived on the Church's land, and the abbots' and bishops' soldiers fought for the King:

❝ *William, King of the English, to Aethelwig, Abbot of Evesham*
Greeting, I order you to summon all those who are subject to your rule and law that they bring before me at Clarendon on the Octave of Pentecost all the knights they owe me duly equipped. You, also that day shall come to me, and bring with you fully equipped those five knights which you owe me in terms of your abbacy. Witness Eudo the Steward, at Winchester. ❞ (**B**)

When William became king the English church was in the hands of Anglo-Saxons. Soon William put his own men in as abbots and bishops. The most famous was Lanfranc, the new Archbishop of Canterbury, **C**. William chose some bishops because they were holy men, others because they were his close friends and good soldiers. The most famous fighting bishop was William's half-brother Odo, every inch a soldier. Try and find a picture of him on the Bayeux tapestry - he will be armed to the teeth!

The Normans built many new cathedrals and churches like **D** which gives a good idea of their round arches and windows and solid walls and pillars. You might even find these design features in one of your local churches.

Only men could be priests. The bishops had to work very hard to make sure that priests did not break their holy vows or promises to serve God, and God only. In 1102 the Archbishop of Canterbury laid down strict rules for priests:

> 1 *Priests should no longer have wives.*
> 2 *No priest shall work for the government, nor be judge of life and death.*
> 3 *Priests shall not spend time in pubs.*
> 4 *They should dress in clothes of one colour and simple clothes.*
> 5 *No church office shall be sold.*
> 6 *No tithe should be given to anyone not a priest.*
> 7 *Abbots shall not be knights or men of war.*
> 8 *Abbots shall sleep and eat in their abbeys.*
> 9 *Those with long hair shall have it cut and rounded so that part of their ears can be seen.*
> 10 *Men shall no longer be bought and sold as was the custom in England like cows and oxen.*
> (E)
>
> (Rules for priests, 1102)

Turn to page 80 for a game which shows you what life was like for a Norman priest.

The Norman Church Game

You can prepare and play a card game for two players to see how the Norman church worked. Use the information on pages 78-79 to complete the game.

a Quiz (AT3). Sort out these facts. You can do it as a quiz.
- Who was the Pope?
- What were a bishop, an abbot, a monk and a nun?
- What was a see?
- When you died what would happen to you if you had been evil? (Study **A** with care.)
- What jobs might a bishop or abbot have to do? (Make sure you read **B** as well as the text.)
- What does how Lanfranc looks, **C**, suggest about the kind of person he was?
- How did William I run the church?
- Why might the Normans have built churches in the way which **D** suggests?
- If a priest broke the rules in list **E**, which do you think would be the worst crime? Put list **E** into a new order of crimes, the least bad first, the worst last.

b Making the Game (AT1).
For the game you have to prepare a pack of cards. **F** shows you what a card is like.

> You have been caught in a pub. All priests are banned from pubs and if caught will be fined heavily. If you are caught a second time you will be put in the stocks as well as fined. Should you sin a third time you will be forced to leave the church. Cases are heard in the Bishop's Court.
> Fines for the first offence (in modern money) are:
>
> Bishop   50p
> Priest   20p } paid to the bishop
> Monk   30p
> Nun   40p
>
> **F**

You will have to prepare a card for each of the points set out in **E**. **Split the work up among class members.**
Cards should describe • what happens • how you might gain or lose money, your job and land etc • what punishment you may have to endure.
Fold a piece of A4 paper or card into 8 rectangles, a rectangle for each card.

A card should be prepared for each of the points in **E**, plus cards for each of these points:

1 A church is to be founded in Newton, see page 56. The bishop and priest have to pay for it.
2 An order has come from Judhael, page 58, for two knights to go and fight for him. Bishop gets money from the priest, monk and nun.
3 The building of a new church is costing much more than you had thought. The priest pays a lot of money.
4 A monastery with strict rules is to be founded where you live. The monks pay.
5 William has removed the local Saxon bishop and put a Norman bishop in his place.
6 A new Norman priest has arrived. The old Saxon church has been knocked down. Bishop and priest pay to build a new church.
7 You are going on crusade to win back the Holy Land from the Muslims.

c To Play (AT1). Toss a coin twice to see which character you will take. If H = Heads, T = Tails, then • HH = Bishop • HT = Priest • TH = Monk • TT = Nun. Shuffle the cards and place them face down.
1 In alphabetical order of your name take a card.
2 Read it out.
3 Place it on the bottom of the pack.
4 The next player takes the next card.

d Diary (AT1). Keep a chronicle of what happens to you - each card you take represents one year. Every year you get 50p from the people, but you may have to pay some of it out. Keep an account of how much money you have each year.

The Friar

Most monks and nuns did little to help the poor peasants and town folk learn about Jesus Christ and Christianity. To fill this gap, by the year 1300 a new religious order of **friars**, the Franciscans had been founded. They preached about God in both villages and towns.

Friars moved from place to place, holding meetings, preaching, teaching, praying and hearing the confessions of those who had sinned. **A** shows friars teaching, while **B** shows a friar hearing the confession of a nun.

Friars took a vow (promised God) to live in poverty, and to survive they relied upon gifts of food and clothes. Soon nobles, knights and rich merchants gave them land and money to build hostels where they could stay on their travels. In almost every medieval town, you would find a friary.

What were the main things that a friar believed in?

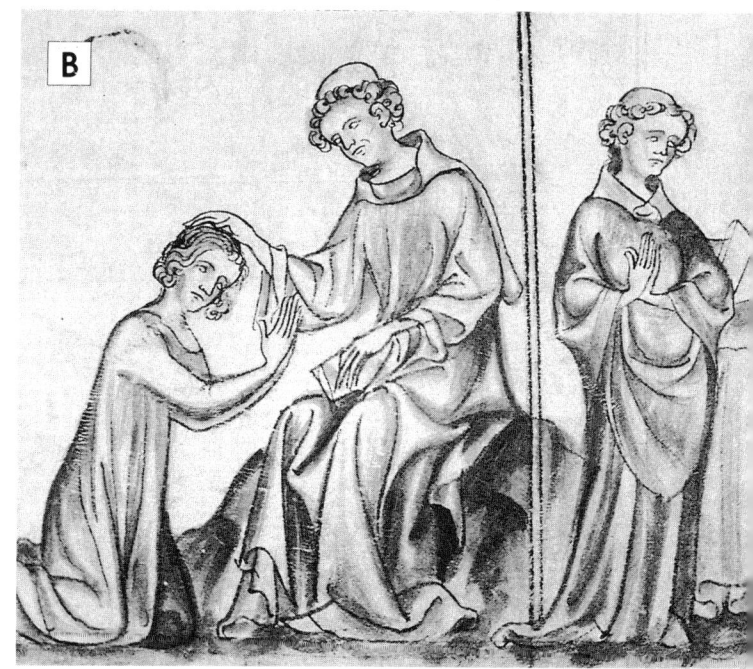

A modern-day Friar (AT1, AT3)

The friars' orders survive today. Produce a story for your school magazine about a visit from a friar who will preach in assembly. Your story could take the form of an interview, or be an advert for his visit. It should say:

- Who the Friar is
- Why he became a friar
- What he believes in
- What he can tell you about what is going on in picture **A**
- What he does
- How he might explain what is going on in picture **B** (Look at his vows!)
- How he looks
- What his life is like

1 Peace at all times
2 Preaching and teaching each day
3 Obeying the head of their order
4 Owning no goods or money
5 Not taking gifts of money
6 Their only clothes should be a gown, cape, belt and sandals
7 They should pass a test before they went preaching
8 They should never talk to women or enter a nunnery

The Priest

The village of Newton had a Norman priest, Orderic. Rainald had sent for Orderic to come from the monastery where Rainald had lived in Normandy. What jobs did Orderic have to do?

> **A Orderic's jobs**
> - hold church services each day and twice on Sundays. Source **B** gives an idea of a medieval church service. The priest would speak in Latin, the Church's official language.
> - baptise, marry and bury villagers, and give them the last rites as they were dying.
> - help look after the sick, the old, the dying and anyone else who could not make their own living. The Church had to give them food and find somewhere for them to live.

The villagers believed in a God who had total power over their lives. So, Orderic prayed for God's help to make sure that the sick got better and that disease, rain and gales did not destroy the village's crops.

How might Orderic have spent his day?

After he had put on his richly embroidered cloak and sandals, and combed his long hair he went to the wooden church to hold a service, **B**, and say mass. **B** is a much later picture, but gives an idea of how he might have looked. After morning service John Fuller came to ask Orderic to pray to God to forgive John his sin of stealing Rainald's fish from the fishpond - see page 65.

Orderic went back to his hut which he shared with Mary, the daughter of Margaret Robberts, and their nine children. **C** gives a lovely idea of medieval family life. Mary gave Orderic his breakfast of milk and coarse brown bread, and he then hurried to the site of the new church. Rainald had given Odo, his reeve, orders to build a new church. The gang of peasants, **D**, were hard at work building a brand new stone church like **D** on page 79. When it was finished, the gang would pull down the old timber Saxon church. John Rogers the Mason and Orderic talked about how they would plan the inside of the new building. After a quick lunch of fish, ale and bread in Margaret Robberts' ale house Orderic visited peasants who needed his help and advice.

Orderic then visited Rainald to plan a church service and feast to give thanks for the harvest, which was almost over. Orderic was pleased that the harvest had gone well. The 50 strips which he held as the Church's own land, the **glebe**, had yielded a bumper crop. Also, he knew that the tenth of their goods which the peasants had to give him, the Church's **tithe**, would fill his tithe barn to the roof.

D

E The Peasants' needs
- Joan Lawe, sister of John Lawe the carpenter. Her husband has broken his leg and cannot work. She has four young children and no food in the house.
- Mark Everard, John Everard's father, has died.
- Anne and Peter Lee have just had a baby daughter.
- John Spenser and Mark Waugh have just agreed that their son Lepsi and daughter June shall marry.
- John Law, his wife and three children have all been struck down with a terrible sickness. Orderic thinks it might be plague.

The Medieval Priest

Write, rehearse and act or tape record a class play about a day in the life of a medieval village priest. Your programme will follow the events of Orderic's day. But it can also home in on the different things that the priest does. Give the roles of Orderic, Rainald, Odo and peasants to class members. Do **a**, then split up the jobs **b-g** among you.

a A timetable (AT1). Make out a timetable of the things that Orderic might do from getting up to going to bed.
b His home, dress, services (AT3). Talk to Orderic about what he wears (**B**) and why; about his home (**C**) and about his church services, **F**.
c The old church (AT1). Interview peasants about what they think and feel about the old church being pulled down, the sacking of their old priest and the work they have to do for Rainald, Odo and Orderic, see pages 62-63.
d The new church, D (AT1). A talk between Orderic and John the Mason about how the building is going and their plans for the inside of the church.
e The peasants' needs (AT2). What should Orderic do about each of the cases in **E**? Look carefully at Orderic's duties, **A**, before deciding what to do.
f The bishop's orders (AT1, AT3). The bishop's orders, see page 79, have arrived. Interview Orderic about what he intends to do about them.
g Interview peasants (AT1). Interview the peasants about why they think it is important to have a priest and church in the village What order would they put these reasons in? They all believe in God - They need the priest to look after them - The church is at the centre of village life.

ACTIVITY ACTIVITY

F Church services
(average 30 minutes each)

Prime	6.30 am	None	2.00 pm
Terce	9.00 am	Vespers	6.00 pm
Sept	12.00 am	Compline	8.30 pm

Monks and Nuns

Near my home is a monastery, Buckfast Abbey, **A**. A monk, Father Vonier, founded and built it, because he wanted to thank God for saving his life when the ship he was in sank. Father Vonier got other monks to join him, and they trained themselves to do all the work needed to build the monastery. This monastery, founded in 1906, is the newest in England. It is an amazing living monument to the faith and driving energy of one man.

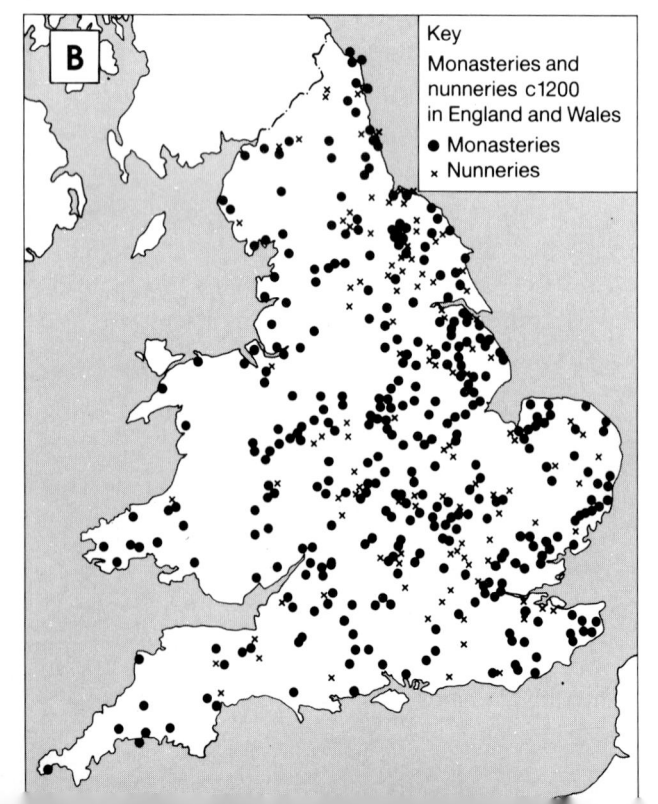

Between 950-1250 such acts of faith were common right across Europe. Men and women set up thousands of monasteries and nunneries which grew quickly, **B**. Monks and nuns would often leave their own monastery or nunnery to found a new one, rather like a swarm of bees flying off to found a new hive. In time a monastic **order** would grow up which looked a bit like a family tree.

What did it mean to be a monk or nun? Most obeyed a set of rules in the same way you do when you become a brownie, cub, guide or scout. The rules most monks and nuns followed were those of St. Benedict (**C**).

> *Rules of St. Benedict*
> *1 When you enter the nunnery (monastery) you stay there until you die.*
> *2 All sisters (brothers) take turns in the kitchens and help each other, so no one gets out of doing kitchen work.*
> *3 Nuns (monks) shall be silent at all times, especially at night, unless they have to speak.*
> *4 The Abbess (Abbot) shall call all the nuns (monks) to a meeting to decide on what to do.*
> *5 They shall quickly obey the abbess' (abbot's) orders.*
> *6 A mattress, blanket, pillow and sheet are enough for a bed.*
> *7 Nuns (monks) shall sleep in their own beds.*
> *8 Nuns (monks) shall sleep in their cloaks.*
> *9 Let a candle always burn at night.*
> *10 No one shall own a thing.*
> *11 Nuns (monks) shall pray eight times a day.*
> *12 At every meal there shall be a reading from the bible.* (**C**)

The monks and nuns wore simple clothes, **D**, often having a rough, itchy hair shirt next to their skin to make them suffer. Can you think why? Monks cut their hair in a special

D

way to remind them of the crown of thorns which Christ wore on The Cross. Both monks and nuns would spend most of their time in prayer or in studying The Bible.

Life was simple and hard. Why did men and women live this way? Ailred of Rievaulx, a famous monk gives us a fascinating peep into the monk's mind when he tells us :

66 We have little food, our clothes are rough, our drink is from the stream and our sleep often upon our book. Under our tired limbs there is but a hard mat; when sleep is sweetest we must rise at a bell's bidding. Self-will has no part to play, there is no moment to be idle or play. Everywhere peace, everywhere stillness and peace of mind, and a marvellous freedom from the hurly burly of the world. 99 **(E)**

(Ailred of Rievaulx c1135 *The Monastic order of England*)

Monastic Quiz

Opinion polls are part of all our lives. You can take part in an opinion poll on monastic life, and make up your own questions for one.

a Opinion Poll (AT1). Write out the questions in the top list and choose which you think is the right answer from the bottom list. Then ask an adult the questions, and write down their answers. As a form pool the replies, and see what grown-ups know about monks and nuns !

Questions
1   Why did the monks wear plain sandals?
2   Why did monks have their heads shaved and a ring of hair around the bald patch?
3   What did monks and nuns sleep in or on ?
4   When could they speak ?
5   How long did monks or nuns have to stay in the monastery ?
6   Why did they wear a cross on their belts?
7   How many times a day did they have to pray ?
8   They mainly studied which book or books ?
9   What could they own ?
10   Why were their cloaks and hoods of thick, itchy cloth?

Possible Answers
1   • never • all the time • when they had to
2   • nothing • their clothes and bible • a retirement cottage
3   • the psalms • the bible • the old testament
4   • feather beds • the floor • a hard mattress
5   • 6 • 8 • 10
6   to remind them of Christ's bare feet
7   to remind them of Christ's crown of thorns
8   to remind them of Christ's crucifixion
9   to make them suffer in the same way that Christ suffered
10   • 10 • 20 • 30 years or for life

b Interviewing Ailred (AT2, AT1).
If you were to interview Ailred as part of your poll, what could he tell you about his life as a monk? Use the Sources to work out your questions.
Questions on:
Source **A** On what the monastery was like
Source **C** On what it was like to live under the order of St Benedict
Source **D** On how he dressed, and why
Source **E** On what went on in his mind in a normal day of praying, reading and working.

ACTIVITY · ACTIVITY ·

Monastery!

Can you think what it would be like to move home, if instead of going to a new house or flat, you end up in the middle of a forest clearing with all your things? When monks founded a new monastery they faced this kind of problem, as a chronicle extract I found, **A**, tells us:

> *Abbot Gerald and his monks were travelling from Furness with nothing except the books and luggage which they could take on a cart drawn by eight oxen.* **(A)**

Abbot Gerald was looking for a place to found a new monastery. Dressed in a white robe, he was a white monk, a member of the Cistercian order which was named after the Abbey of Citeaux where it was set up. The Cistercians believed in possessing nothing more than they needed to survive. They aimed to live and suffer like Christ when he went to live in the desert wilderness with hardly any food. The poorer, tougher and harsher the site for their new home, the better.

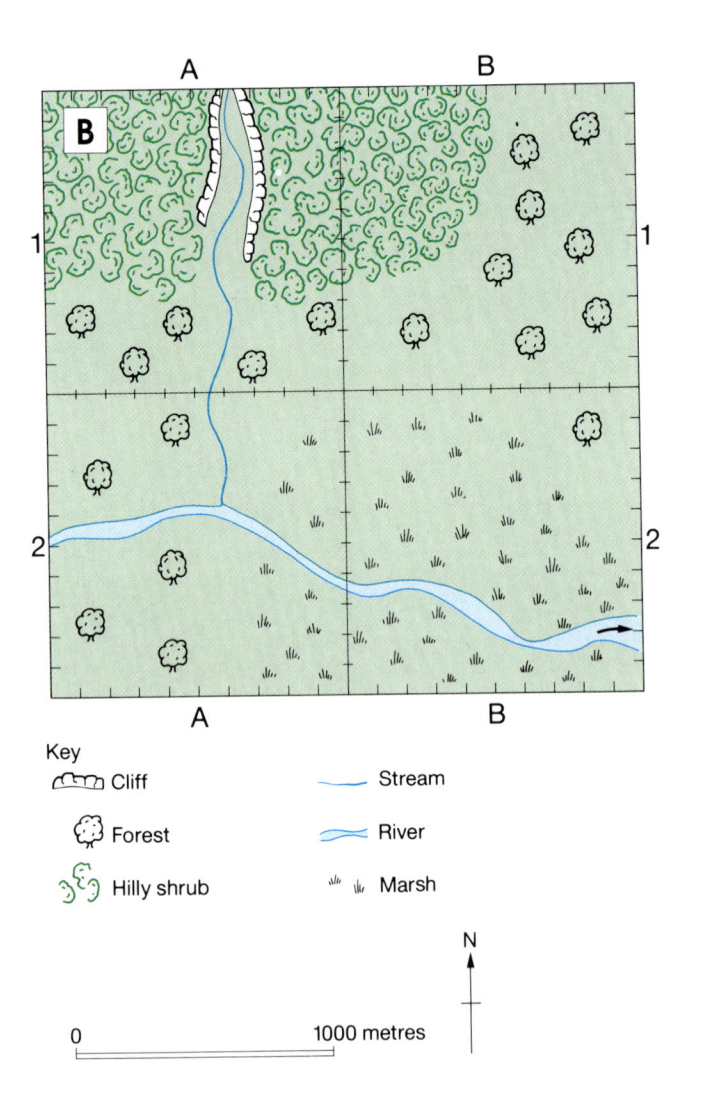

Key
- Cliff
- Forest
- Hilly shrub
- Stream
- River
- Marsh

0 — 1000 metres

Building a monastery

How well do you think you would do as a Cistercian monk if you had to choose a site for a monastery and then plan and build it? Map **B** shows the place where you will found your monastery. Rainald, the lord who owns the land, says you can settle there. Below are lists of choices you can make. Call a meeting of the monks to discuss and decide what to do. This we call the chapter meeting. After each choice write down what you have decided to do, and mark it on the plan.

The Monastic Site - Decision 1

You need to choose two squares which are side by side - A1/B1, A1/A2, B1/B2, A2/B2. Which two squares next to each other will you choose?

You will need somewhere which

- has poor soil,
- is cut off,
- is flat for the monastery buildings,
- has some land on which to grow crops and raise animals.

Write down the squares, and give your reasons for picking them.

Having chosen your monastery site, enlarge it. Begin to keep a diary or a chronicle of the story of your monastery. After each choice carry on with your chronicle - put in dates.

Settling the Monastery - Decision 2

Now you have to decide what to do next. Will you:
- **2a** Clear forest - plant crops
- **2b** Drain marsh
- **2c** Clear the site for a church
- **2d** Ask for a gift of 100 sheep

Say which TWO of these things you will do. THEN look at the decision table on page 88.

C

Settling the Monastery - Decision 3

a Clear forest - plant crops
b Drain marsh
c Clear the site for a church
d Ask for a gift of 100 sheep
e Begin to quarry rock for the new church

Say which two NEW things you will now do. THEN look at the decision table on page 88.

Building the Monastery - Decision 4

You now push on with the building of the monastery. Which part of the monastery will you build first?

4a The church - Plan the church. Look at page 78 for ideas.

4b Design a window. (You could use windows in your local church as a guide.)
4c The refectory (the kitchens and monks' dining room).
4d The dormer, where the monks sleep.

Mark your choice on your plan, following the pattern on the map on page 86. Now look at the decision table on page 88.

Building the Monastery - Decisions 5, 6, 7

You go on with the building of the monastery. You make new choices from the list. Mark them on your plan, following the pattern on the map on page 86. After each choice is made, look at the decision table on page 88. Describe how the building is going, using what you can see in **C** to help you. Talk about what you can see

Building the Monastery - Decision 8

Now plan out the rest of the monastery like the monk shown in **D** on page 88. **D** is a carving found on a seat in a medieval monastery. **E** is a plan of another monastery nearby. You could copy it or change parts of it.

ACTIVITY

87

D

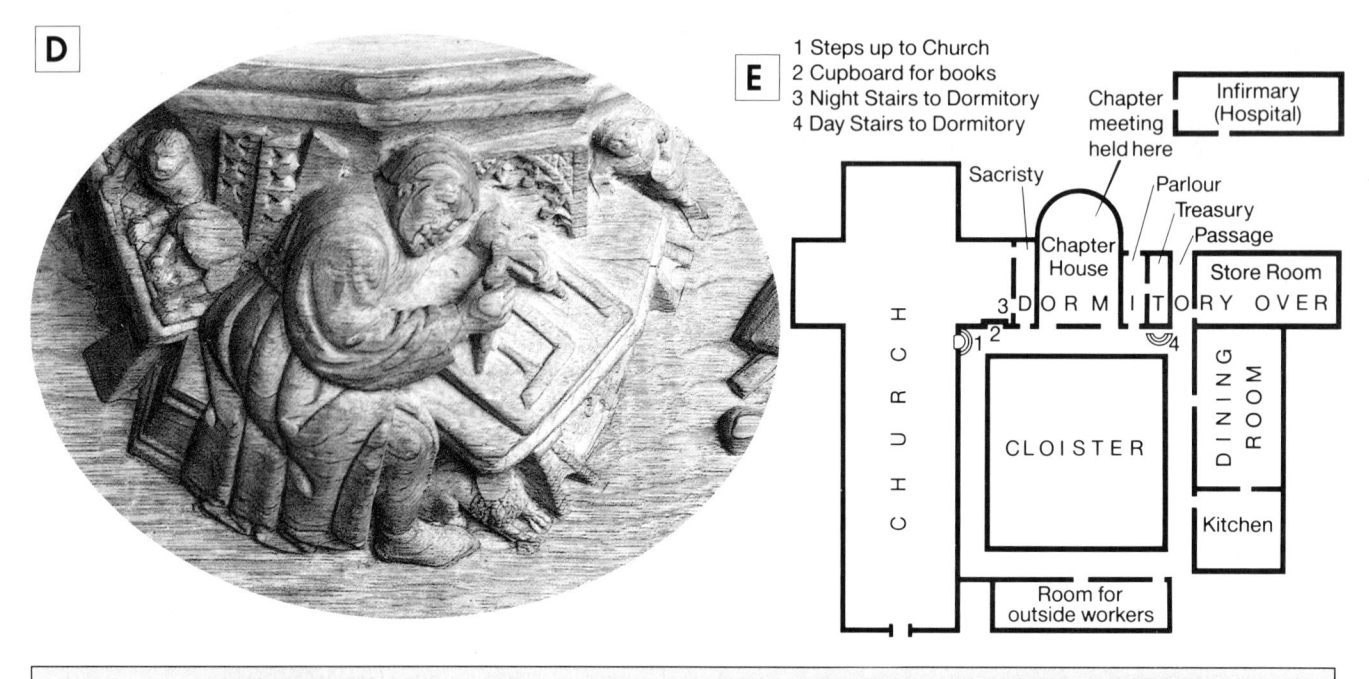

E
1 Steps up to Church
2 Cupboard for books
3 Night Stairs to Dormitory
4 Day Stairs to Dormitory

DECISION TABLE.

1 Look down the table to find each decision you had to make.
2 Then toss a coin to see what happens after each decision you have made.

Clear forest - plant crops

Heads The forest is burned down easily, and the land cleared with axes. The crops grow well, and you have a rich harvest. Ten new monks join you.
Tails You manage to clear the forest, the crops grow well. But, before harvest, fierce storms destroy the crops. Three monks die of starvation.

Drain marsh

Heads The marsh draining goes well. You are able to prepare the foundations for the church.
Tails The marsh is drained, but half way through the work marsh fever sweeps through the monks, two die, the rest cannot do any more work.

Clear the site for a church

Heads You find it very hard to dig foundations in the granite, and the work goes on very slowly.
Tails The baron lends you his serfs to help you, and you manage to get on well with the church foundations.

Ask for a gift of 100 sheep

Heads The sheep enjoy living in the new lands you have cleared, they double in number and you sell their wool to buy tools, glass and food to help build the church.
Tails Foot rot affects the sheep - half of them die. You had hoped to sell the wool to pay for tools.

Begin to quarry rock for the new church

Heads Four of the monks light a bonfire under the cliff face to heat it before pouring on water to split the rock. The fire goes out, they pour on water, there is a rock fall and they are killed.
Tails The cutting and shaping of the rock goes well. A trained mason joins the monks and helps train the monks.

The Church - plan it out and build it

Heads The church is built with great speed. The love which God has shown you helps with the rest of your work.
Tails You work so hard on the church that the rest of the work goes slowly, and many monks are sick through not having anywhere proper to sleep or eat.

The refectory, the kitchens and monks dining room

Heads The kitchens mean the building work can press on much faster.
Tails The work was done so quickly, that one morning you find the whole kitchens have collapsed in rubble.

The dormer, where the monks sleep

Heads The dormer is only half built when a storm floods it, most of the monks catch a fever, and three die.
Tails Somewhere dry to sleep is a great help - the monks are now much more healthy, and they can press on with their building and study of the Bible.

The Monastic School

How would you like to go to a school where you arrive with your parents and:

“Let the parents bring the boy/girl to the altar and wrap his/her right hand in the altar cloth. Then, having kissed it, let them put it into the hands of the monk who is looking after the boy/girl, and make the sign of the cross over his/her head. Then let the Abbott/Abbess pour holy water on the boy's/girl's head.” (A)

Your hair would be cut, **B**. If you were a boy it would be **tonsured** [cut in a ring], to remind you of Christ's crown of thorns. Then you would change from your own clothes into the gown of a novice monk or nun, and you would be left with the monk or nun who would be looking after you.

The monastic school would have a single monk or nun in charge. All of your lessons would teach you how to be a servant of God. You would have to learn to read - in Latin - for the main book which you would study would be the Bible. The Bible was written in Latin, and you would use Latin to read other religious books as well. You would also have to learn the church services (see page 83) and how to sing and chant psalms and prayers. You would be taught how to write, and in time you might become a skilled illuminator of religious books. Remember that all books were hand copied at this time, for there was no printing. As well as your lessons you would learn a craft, such as being a mason, brewing, farming, weaving or carpentry. The monks had to make all the goods they needed. Life was strict, and if you were naughty you might be caned, **C**.

A Day at School

a Timetable (AT1).

- Work out the timetable of lessons you have today. What subjects do you have and how long do they last? Put in breaks, meal times and homework. Mention any cases where a pupil disobeys a teacher, and how he or she is punished.

- Work out the kinds of things you might have learned in the monastery school. Draw up a timetable allowing the same amount of time for each subject. Allow time for meals and church services (see page 83). Mention any cases where a pupil disobeys a teacher, and how he or she is punished.

b Interview (AT1).

In pairs, take the roles of a novice monk or nun, and interview each other about how you spend the day in the monastery school. The interviewer can then ask you about the main similarities and differences between the monastic school and modern school life.

The Medieval Doctor

You fall ill. You go to the doctor - but he has no modern drugs and medicines and does not know that germs and viruses cause disease. The doctor thinks that the body is made up of four humours - earth, fire, water and air. If these humours should get out of balance you fall ill (**A**). The weather could have a big impact on the balance of humours in your body. In summer the dry heat would increase the fire. So, you would sweat and get very hot. You might even become bad tempered - choleric. What might happen in winter?

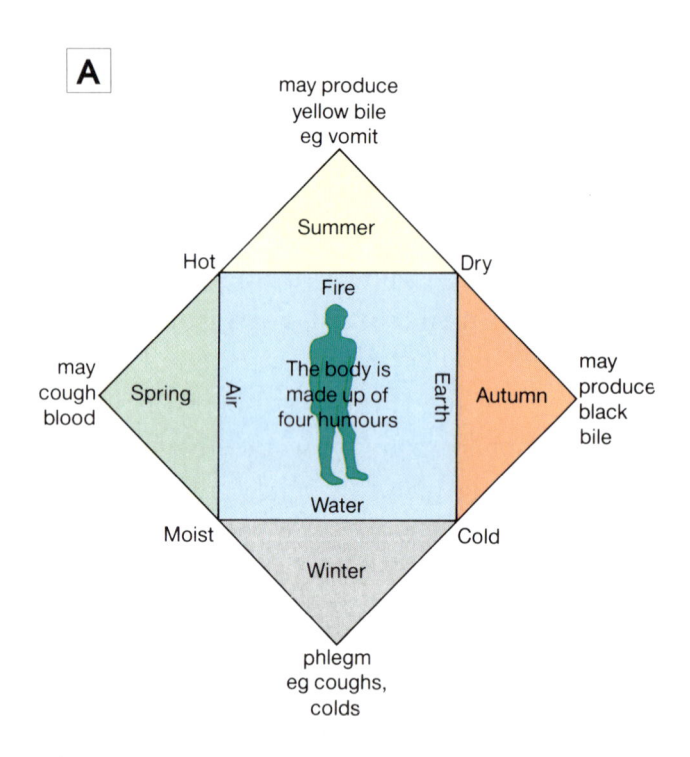

A

- Summer — may produce yellow bile eg vomit
- Hot / Dry
- Fire (top), Earth (right), Water (bottom), Air (left)
- The body is made up of four humours
- Spring — may cough blood
- Autumn — may produce black bile
- Moist / Cold
- Winter — phlegm eg coughs, colds

To find out what is wrong with you, your doctor would feel your pulse and look at your urine and tongue (**B**). One way of getting the humours back into balance would be to bleed you. Another would be to give you a special kind of drink. I chose the medieval cures in Source **C** to suggest how the theory of humours worked. They also show the ghastly ways in which doctors treated patients!

B

> **Lumbago (back ache)** Two pennyweights of betony (a herb) and two bowlfuls of sweet wine mixed with hot water. Give to a patient while fasting.
>
> **Tuberculosis (lung disease)** Smear the man with oil and warm the sides and the ribs with new wool, and between the shoulders, a little before evening. Then let the oil remain on him. After that, bleed him from the elbow in an oven where the fire cannot harm him. If you let him give too much blood there will be no hope of his life.
>
> **Asthma** Put the lung of a fox into sweetened wine and drink the mixture.
>
> **Sore eyelid** Poke the sore with nine grains of barley and say: flee, flee, barley chase you.
>
> **Toothache** Burn to ashes the teeth of a dog. Heat a cupful of wine, put the dust in, and drink. Do so often, and the teeth will be better.

(**C**)

Medieval doctors were highly skilled - they had worked out ways of treating sprains and broken bones (**D**). You might also be well looked after in a nunnery where the nuns worked as nurses (**E**).

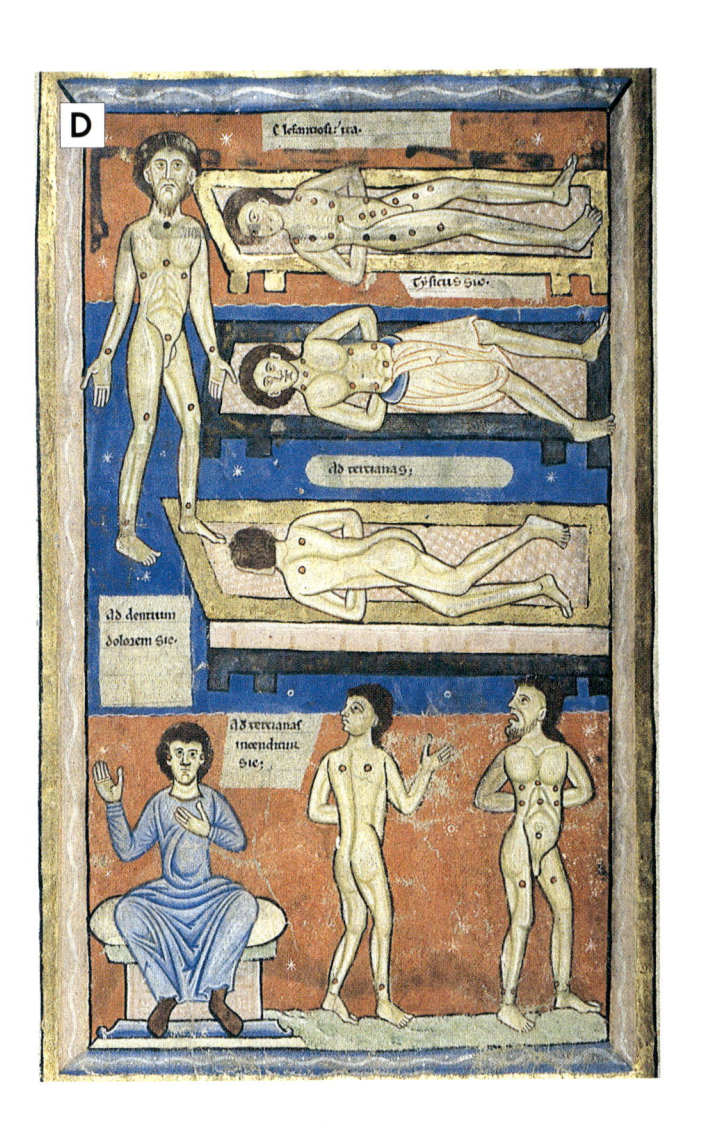

Medieval Clinic (AT2, AT3)

You can work out what it might have been like to have been a medieval doctor, and then hold a surgery for patients. If you work as a group, you can split tasks **b-e** up among you. You can do **f** as a class activity.

a Think hard about **A**. Then say how the body's four humours might be in balance for a healthy person, and what might be wrong with someone:
• who has a high temperature • who is depressed
• whose body becomes covered with oozing boils.

b Study **C**, and then say, as a medieval doctor, what might be wrong with the patients who have lumbago, tuberculosis and toothache, and why the doctor has suggested the cures in **C**.

c Study **D**, and then suggest treatment for a broken foot, a sprained ankle, and a dislocated elbow and shoulder.

d Take four of our most common diseases, and then work out how you would try and cure them as a medieval doctor.

e As a class you can then hold a clinic in which you put forward the different cures you have come up with for illnesses form members have had in the past six months. Tell them what hospital life might be like, see **E**.

f Draw up a table comparing the medieval cures with those which a doctor would suggest today.

ACTIVITY

The Black Death 1348

Each week your local newspaper is full of local stories. How might it report the approach of a new, deadly disease like AIDS? In the Middle Ages, rats brought the **Black Death** to England on ships. **A** shows how disease spread.

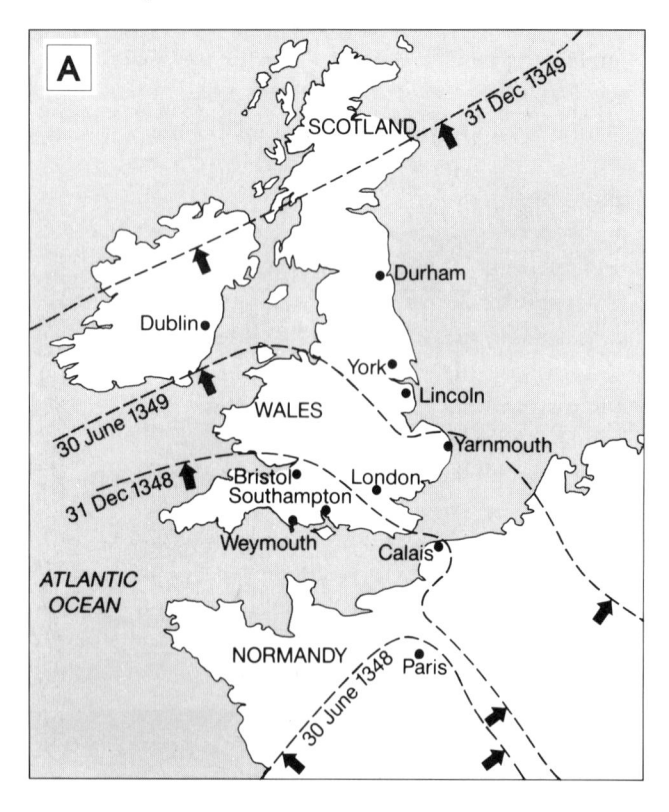

[A] Map showing spread of the Black Death across Britain and northern France, with dates: 30 June 1348, 31 Dec 1348, 30 June 1349, 31 Dec 1349. Locations marked: Scotland, Dublin, Durham, York, Lincoln, Wales, Yarmouth, Bristol, Southampton, London, Weymouth, Calais, Normandy, Paris, Atlantic Ocean.

I chose **B** because it suggests what men and women thought and feared about the Black Death. The figure at the back isn't a medieval policeman keeping football hooligans in control! Groups such as the one in **B** roamed far and wide in search of God's help against the Black Death. As they walked along they beat themselves and each other with a whip or scourge, howling and crying as the blood flowed down their backs. We call such people flagellants. Source **C** is my account of the Black Death or plague, I based it on what I read in History textbooks and in books on the history of medicine.

> *Today we know that a germ caused the Black Death or plague. Fleas carried on rats spread the plague. Medieval people thought that they caught plague by breathing it in from the air. Plague took two forms. One form, **pneumonic plague**, affected the lungs, while the other, **bubonic plague**, caused large boils to appear on the body. Pneumonic plague killed you as you coughed up your diseased lungs. You would have had some hope of getting better from bubonic plague.* **(C)**

(Jon Nichol, 1990)

In **D** a medieval doctor gives us a gruesome cure for the Black Death. But look at page 90 to see what might have been behind the doctor's cure - it is not as daft as it seems.

> *Toads should be thoroughly dried in the air or sun. They should be laid on the boil. Then the toad will swell and draw the poison of the plague through the skin to its own body. When it is full, it should be thrown away and a new one applied.* **(D)**

(Anon c 1350)

First catch your toad! Another doctor worked out that the best way to treat bubonic plague was to slice open the boils and burn them out with a red hot poker. Again, look at pages 90-91 to work out why he thought this would cure the plague.

E

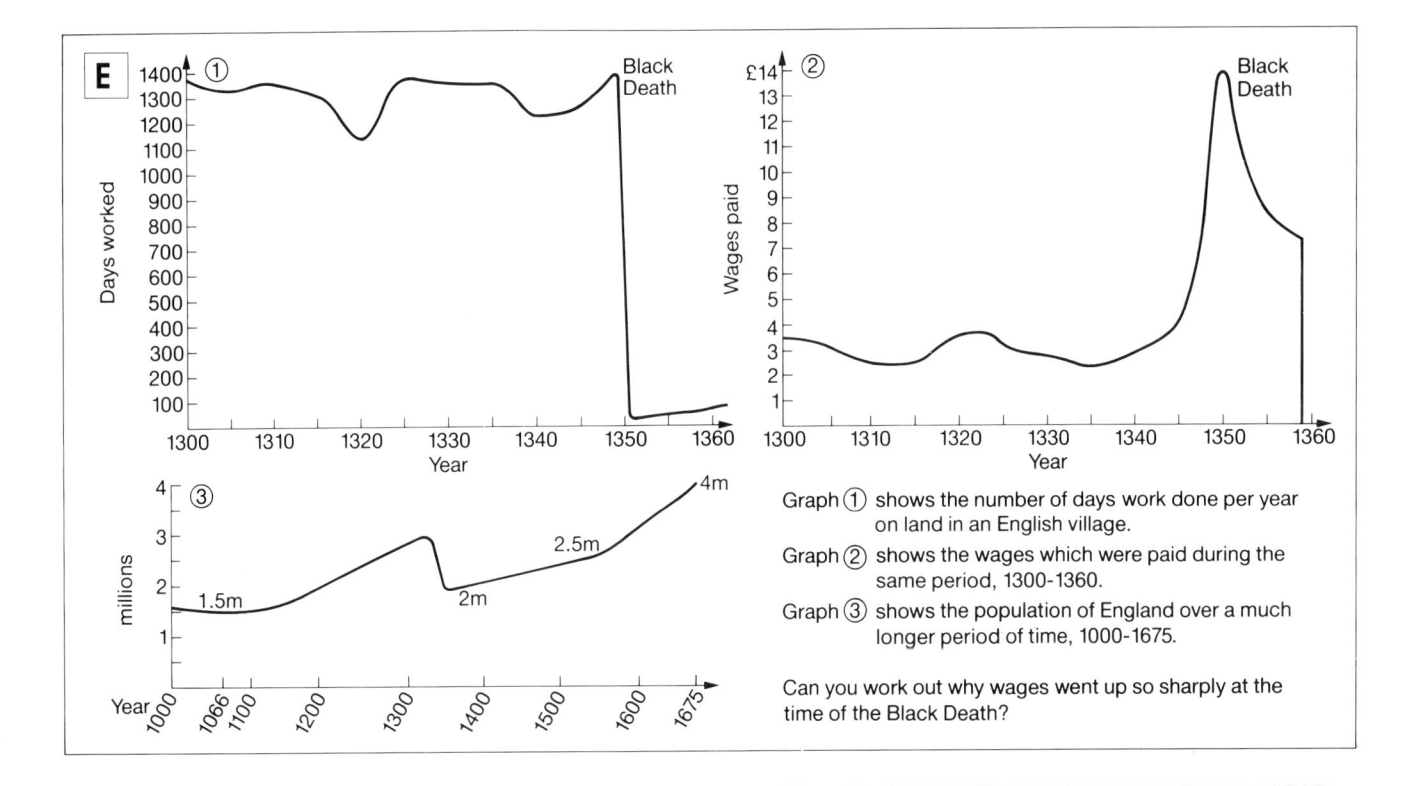

Graph ① shows the number of days work done per year on land in an English village.

Graph ② shows the wages which were paid during the same period, 1300-1360.

Graph ③ shows the population of England over a much longer period of time, 1000-1675.

Can you work out why wages went up so sharply at the time of the Black Death?

Black Death Reporter

When you leave school you might get a job as a young reporter. Your editor has sent you off to find out about the spread of a dreadful disease, the Black Death, which has reached your town and local villages. You have a file with stories, pictures and facts in it, including sources **A-E**.

You can split the work up among you, working by yourselves, in pairs or groups. The stories could form a class display.

a Local Report (AT1, AT3). Write a report on the impact of the Black Death on the area where you live. Hold interviews with the following people. Use their replies to write your report.
- The local chief of police. Where has the disease come from?
- A doctor. What are the symptoms of the disease? How long does it last? What cures are there?
- A flagellant. Why are you a member of this group of flagellants? What happened to your family? What are you doing to yourself and why?
- A shop keeper. She has had the disease and her family died. What did she do when members of her family fell ill, with pus oozing out of black boils the size of hens' eggs in their armpits and their groins?
- A local priest. He is one of the few priests to have survived.
- The scene in the village, which is almost totally deserted. People have fled in panic.

b The editor's comments (AT2).

Most papers contain the views of the editor in what is called a leader column. Write such a leader called Impact of The Black Death. Before you start, read through the consequences below. Then decide whether you are on the landowners' side or on the side of the peasants. Write your leader from one of their points of view.

- Deserted villages, crumbling huts, deserted, derelict churches and halls.
- Crops rotting in the fields, farm animals running wild, fields turning back into wilderness.
- Not enough farm labourers left to work the land, and run the estates of rich landowners.
- The effect on wages (see **E**). Why do you think wages changed in this way?
- Demands from labourers that they should stop being slaves or serfs, owned by their local landlord and working for a roof over their heads and enough food to eat. They demanded that they should become free men who owned their own land and worked for whoever would give them the highest wages.
- Landowners felt that God was punishing them for their greed.

What do you think?

Crime and Punishment

'How do you plead, guilty or not guilty?' the judge asked John Rogers at his medieval trial for murder. When you grow up you may well have to be a member of a jury which decides whether a prisoner is guilty of a crime. A judge would hear the case and advise the jury. The way we try cases grew up in the Middle Ages, although both the courts and the punishments are different now.

How would a royal judge have tried a murder case? How would Rainald, Eleanor and John and Mary Fuller have decided in the manor court who had the right to graze their cow in the meadow, or how to punish the village drunkard? To help you think about how you would have tried medieval cases, read through the notes below.

The King The King would often judge major cases himself, eg a lord who had rebelled against him, or a row over who owned a castle (**A**). Or, he might hand the cases over to his royal judges to try in the King's courts.

The King's Judges The King's judges would also travel to county courts to try cases such as murder, or non-payment of the King's taxes.

The Manor Court Below the county court were local courts, the manor courts. The manor court of Newton handled cases such as drunkenness, the payment of fines for a marriage and the straying of sheep and cows into a neighbour's strips.

The Town Court Towns also had their own courts like the Manor Courts. Punishments were often harsh, see **B** and Fact file **C**.

Trying Cases There were three other ways of trying cases apart from getting the King or his judges to decide.

Trial by Combat In cases where there was a row between two nobles like Judhael or Earl Roger they could demand a trial by combat. The nobles, or champions they hired, would fight to see who was guilty. God would show who was guilty - the winner would be telling the truth!

Trial by Ordeal You could choose to grip a red hot poker or be thrown into a pond to see if you sank or floated. In the case of the poker, if the wound healed, God would show that you were innocent. You were also supposed to be innocent if you sank!

Trial by Jury Cases in the Manor Court would have a jury of up to twelve freemen, with the Lord or Lady or their reeve in charge.

The Hue and Cry If you spotted a thief, you were supposed to raise the hue and cry - that is, shout 'thief, thief' and chase after him with as many people as you could get to help, a bit like a Wild West posse.

FACTFILE

C Medieval punishments

Treason - trying to kill or depose the king Draw through the streets on a hurdle. Hang until half dead, rip out the guts and burn them, behead. Place the head on a spike, and cut the body in four pieces to place on the town's four maingates.
Rebellion against the king Hang from trees and gallows
Fighting and wounding A heavy fine or placed in the stocks or pillory
Preaching against the teaching of the Pope - Heresy Burn at the stake
Stealing, burgling Fine 40s for a weekday, £4 for a Sunday
Rape Fine 40s for a weekday, £4 for a Sunday
Failure to raise the hue and cry Fine, 10s for a freeman, 20s for a knight
False weights and measures 4s fine
False coins and forgery Castration and loss of the right hand
Selling bread with chalk dust in it The pillory
Telling lies The pillory
Selling bad beer The ducking stool
Nagging The ducking stool

The Medieval Court (AT1)

We can hold a medieval trial. Or, you can work out what punishments you would hand out for the cases listed below tried in either a Town or a Manor Court. For each case you can write down what you know on a piece of paper. When the case is tried read it out as a witness. Then you can do this again, having heard what other witnesses have had to say.

1 You can all be a member of the jury.
2 Each case can call witnesses who can tell what they know about the cases.
3 After each case make an entry on the Manor Court Roll of what you decide, and the punishment, if any.

The Cases
- **Margaret Robberts**, accused of nagging her husband so that he has left home: he now lives with John Skep's daughter in a hovel on the common.
- **John Spenser**, for breaking into the mill and stealing a bag of corn. The village constable found the corn in his hut.
- **Mark Waugh**, for fighting with John Lawe after an evening in the ale house. John Lawe's wife complained to the constable after her husband came home with a black eye and cut lip in the morning.
- **John Smith**, who has been found coining false money. The dies for making the money were buried under the floor of his smithy.
- **John Rogers** is accused of murder. Baldric the butcher was found murdered in his shop with a dagger thrust between his shoulders. Baldric's wife, Constance, says that she recognises the dagger - it is John Rogers'. Earlier John and Baldric had been drinking in the Black Pig with Cerdric and David, and their girl friends Margaret and Emma. A row broke out over some money that Baldric claimed that John Rogers owed him. The town watch, Etheldred, Gospric and Hereward broke up the fight and took John Rogers and Baldric to the town jail. In jail they talked to Jane, Gillian and Margaret who were under arrest for street walking and stealing purses. John Rogers and Baldric were released when sober. John Rogers' wife, Matilda, says he went straight home to bed and they were woken up by the watch who arrested him for murder. Matilda had spent the night making black pudding from the blood of a pig they had killed that day, so there was blood all around the house and on John Rogers' clothes.

ACTIVITY

Norman French and English

> *Bifil that in that seson on a day,*
> *In Southwerk at the Tabard as I lay*
> *Redy to wenden on my pilgrymage*
> *To Caunterbury with ful devout corage,*
> *At nyght was come into that hostelrye*
> *Wel nyne and twenty in a compaignye,*
> *Of sondry folk, by aventure yfalle*
> *In felaweshipe, and pilgrimes were*
> *they alle,*
> *That toward Caunterbury wolden ryde.*
> *The chambres and the stables weren wyde,*
> *And wel we weren esed atte beste.*
> *And shortly, when the sonne was to reste,*
> *So hadde I spoken with hem everichon*
> *That I was of hir felaweshipe anon,*
> *And made forward erly for to ryse,*
> *To take oure wey ther as I yow*
> *devyse.* **(A)**

(Geoffrey Chaucer c1390 The Canterbury Tales)

A is part of a poem written in about 1390 AD. By yourself or with a partner, try to work out its meaning. What language is it written in? Is it French or English? The extract is taken from the Prologue or introduction to twenty-four stories written as poems. In Geoffrey Chaucer's *Canterbury Tales* pilgrims told these stories to each other on their pilgrimage from London to Canterbury.

Chaucer (c1340-1400), England's greatest medieval poet, lived and worked at the court of the English king. By then English, and not Norman French, was the court language. We are not sure when or how the Normans changed from speaking French to using English. It must have been a very slow change, over many years. This did not mean that the language of the Normans, French, was swept away. The Normans brought to England many of the words we use today, words like haddock and harness. Other Norman words we use all the time are first names like Richard and Eleanor, and place names. Changing from speaking French to English was one way in which the Normans died out as a race, as a Norman schoolbook pointed out:

> *...now that the English and Normans have lived so long together, and have married one another, the nations have become so mixed together (I speak of freemen only) that we can hardly these days tell apart an Englishman and a Norman.* **(B)**

(c 1180)

Race and Language (AT1, AT3).

All of us are descended from people who came to Britain as immigrants. Try and find out from your first names and surnames, and by asking at home, which country some of your ancestors might have come from and when they came. As a form make out a table like the one below.

FAMILY NAME	COUNTY	DATE OF ARRIVAL	ORIGINAL LANGUAGE

What does this table suggest about how we should treat new arrivals, immigrants, to this country?

ACTIVITY